Praise for *Caring for the Dying*

"A pitch-perfect, accessible book on an otherwise inaccessible subject. Fersko-Weiss's beautiful and poignant stories can be used as road maps not only for clinicians but also for patients, family members, or caregivers who wish to stay connected through to the end of life."
—BJ Miller, MD, assistant clinical professor of medicine at UCSF and attending specialist for the Symptom Management Service of the UCSF Helen Diller Family Comprehensive Cancer Center

"An inspired and practical guide on accompanying those on the precipice of death. Henry reaches into his years of experience to provide the reader with invaluable tools. He focuses in on the essential nonmedical elements that really matter like deep listening, sitting vigil, establishing a calm and receptive environment, and facilitating meaningful rituals. Lots of wisdom in these pages."
—Frank Ostaseski, founder of the Metta Institute, co-founder of the Zen Hospice Project, and author of *Five Invitations: Discovering What Death Can Teach Us About Living Fully*

"An extraordinary contribution to the care of the dying. Through story and instruction, Henry Fersko-Weiss offers his great wisdom on how we can offer meaningful care that can not only ease an individual's dying but provide consolation to family and friends as they cope with grief and loss."
—Kenneth J. Doka, author of *Grief Is a Journey*

"Henry's calm, practical, and pioneering book is an excellent guide for those wishing to learn how to be a *doula* for the dying, whether formal or informal, which will certainly also make them an inspiration for the consciously living. This book should be taken up with great relief to guide us from now, while vibrantly alive, and certainly at the time of transition."
—Robert A. F. Thurman, Jey Tsong Khapa professor of Indo-Tibetan Buddhist Studies at Columbia University and author of *Infinite Life* and *Man of Peace*

"The doula program described here provides skilled, compassionate, mindful presence to people at the end of life and their loved ones, helping guide them to an experience of dying which affirms their lives and enriches the lives of those left behind. I wish all patients had access to this amazing program."

—Leslie Blackhall, MD, section chief for palliative medicine and associate professor of medicine at the University of Virginia School of Medicine

"As a pioneer in the work of improving end-of-life care, Henry Fersko-Weiss has written a remarkable book. Drawing from decades of work with the dying, Fersko-Weiss offers up stories and insights as he humbly chronicles his own journey of crafting a much-needed and innovative approach to end-of-life care. *Caring for the Dying* is medicine for a world where far too many of us experience 'unfortunate' deaths. A must read."

—Amy Wright Glenn, author of *Birth, Breath, and Death: Meditations on Motherhood, Chaplaincy, and Life as a Doula*

"Part guidebook, part memoir, *Caring for the Dying* introduces us to the path of end-of-life doulas who accompany people on their journey from this life, who fulfill our collective commitment to care well for one another through the most difficult and vulnerable times, and bear witness to the inherent worth and dignity of every human being."

—Ira Byock, MD, founder and chief medical officer of the Providence Institute for Human Caring and author of *Dying Well*, *The Four Things That Matter Most*, and *The Best Care Possible*

"This is a necessary book for anyone who cares for others—the living and the dying. As one of the pioneers of our contemporary age, Henry has much to teach us."

—Sensei Koshin Paley Ellison, co-founder and co-executive director of the New York Zen Center for Contemplative Care and co-editor of *Awake at the Bedside: Contemplative Teachings on Palliative and End of Life Care*

"*Caring for the Dying* supports my theory that our death can be designed to reflect special moments, our values, our spiritual briefs and even our personality. The death-doula approach is the bridge that can make death an experience and not just a destination."

—Kimberly C. Paul, chief executive officer of Death by Design and creator of Begin the Conversation

"*Caring for the Dying* will not only become a standard for those wishing to train in the way of the doula. It will be a book that answers questions for those who have been in the presence of death and a sourcebook and support for those who wish to bring such a compassionate and caring role into one of life's most challenging and sacred moments."

—Robert Sachs, LISW, board member of Hospice of San Luis Obispo and author of *Rebirth into Pure Land* and *Perfect Endings*

"Please read this book if you or someone you love may die one day. Sacred moments surrounding the last days of life are explicitly delineated in this easy-to-read book, which is full of stories from the author's experience as a professional doula."

—Roberta Temes, PhD, author of *Living with an Empty Chair: A Guide Through Grief*

"An inspiring and moving collection of end-of-life scenarios illustrating how we can face life's final passage with dignity and thoughtfulness. Fersko-Weiss provides a glimpse at the true meaning of a good death. Essential reading for anyone who wants to create a meaningful experience for themselves or someone they care about."

—Fredda Wasserman, co-author with Norine Dresser of *Saying Goodbye to Someone You Love: Your Emotional Journey Through End of Life and Grief*

"In *Caring for the Dying*, Henry Fersko-Weiss brings the reader into his personal journey in supporting a meaningful way of death and dying and his evolving work in the end-of-life-doula movement. The principles and techniques of an end-of-life doula are interwoven with Henry's experiences in a way that makes this book inspirational and helps lessen the mystery and fear of death for any reader who wishes to face their own death with less fear and a focus on meaning."

—Kris Kington-Barker, executive director of Hospice of San Luis Obispo County

"What inspires Henry's eminently practical book is his well-informed insight that we can live and die knowing that we are part of a larger inclusivity. In vigiling, in legacy work, in his guidance on deep listening, Henry teaches us that our living and our dying weave us to one another."

—Marco Mascarin, PhD, RP, co-founder of the Contemplative End of Life Care program at the Institute of Traditional Medicine

"There is an abundance of literature on death and dying, but there is little that can compare with the poignancy, compassion and wisdom that Henry Fersko-Weiss brings to the subject. Drawing on his vast experience as a death doula, he offers practical information and inspirational anecdotes that serve to guide others in the art of being present and caring for the *person* who is dying. Midwifing death in this way honors the dying person, their life and their legacy. A godsend for anyone who wishes to prepare for their own death or midwife the death of someone they love."

—Michael Barbato, MD, retired palliative care physician, researcher, teacher, and author of *Midwifing Death*

"A thoughtful and instructive text on how doulas can help people die as they would wish and a guide for families as they cope with what may be the most stressful period of their lives. Illustrated by his actual cases and those of fellow doulas, Fersko-Weiss has created a useful resource for consumers and professionals dealing with the complicated topic of death and dying."

—Don Pendley, director of hospice and palliative care at the Home Care and Hospice Association of NJ

"Essential reading for all of humanity. *Caring for the Dying* is life changing in how we view and care for our loved ones as they prepare for their death. Henry's touching stories pull the curtain back to give you an intimate look at what is possible at the end of life."

—Debra Pascali-Bonaro, DONA International doula trainer

"This is a lovely contribution to the growing field of care for the dying—and the dying person's loved ones—with both wisdom and compassion. Arising from the author's intimate experience at the end of life, it offers a caring sensitivity well worth considering."

—Kathleen Dowling Singh, author of *The Grace in Dying, The Grace in Aging,* and *The Grace in Living*

"Caring for a loved one and witnessing the dying process is both an act of courage and a privilege—as painful as the process might be. This book, *Caring for the Dying,* can make all the difference in appreciating the process, recognizing through the many stories how natural death is, and helping ultimately to heal and move forward from loss."

—Judy Tatelbaum, LCSW, grief therapist and author of *The Courage to Grieve* and *You Don't Have to Suffer*

Caring *for*
the Dying

The DOULA
APPROACH *to a*
MEANINGFUL DEATH

HENRY FERSKO-WEISS

Conari Press
An OPEN CENTER Book™

For all the dying people and families who have allowed me to walk alongside them during one of the most intimate and personal journeys they take in life. It has been a profound privilege to serve you and to learn from you. You have transformed my life and given it purpose. I hope this book honors your lives and deaths and, through your examples, helps countless others to experience the deep meaning and great comfort that comes from the doula approach to dying.

This edition first published in 2017 by Conari Press, an imprint of
Red Wheel/Weiser, LLC
With offices at:
65 Parker Street, Suite 7
Newburyport, MA 01950
www.redwheelweiser.com

Copyright © 2017 by Henry Fersko-Weiss

ISBN: 978-1-57324-696-5

Library of Congress Cataloging-in-Publication Data

Names: Fersko-Weiss, Henry, author.
Title: Caring for the dying : the doula approach to a meaningful death / by
   Henry Fersko-Weiss.
Description: Newburyport, MA : Conari Press, an imprint of Red Wheel/
   Weiser, LLC, 2017.
Identifiers: LCCN 2016041229 | ISBN 9781573246965 (6 x 9 tc : alk. paper)
Subjects: LCSH: Terminal care. | Terminally ill--Care. | Doulas.
Classification: LCC R726.8 .F48 2017 | DDC 616.02/9--dc23
LC record available at https://lccn.loc.gov/2016041229

Cover design by Kathryn Sky-Peck
Interior by Howie Severson
Typeset in Warnock Pro

Printed in the United States of America

MP

10 9 8 7 6 5 4 3 2 1

Contents

Preface

Death is like a dark and painful family secret that we try to keep hidden away. If we do think about it, we feel terribly vulnerable. Somehow we believe that not thinking about death will keep us safe, protect us from its truth and even from its inevitability.

The medical system in the United States colludes with us in our avoidance of the subject by continuing to hide death in hospitals and nursing homes. Nearly 70 percent of all deaths still occur in these sterile, depersonalized surroundings. And perhaps a quarter of those people die hooked up to tubes amid the shrill beeping of machines in the ICU. Media coverage of medical research, scientific breakthroughs, and the promise of new treatments encourages us to think that cures for the worst illnesses can occur at any time. As an extreme example of denial, a doctor in the United States established a prize of one million dollars for the person who can successfully "hack the code of life" and defeat death for good.

Our collective fear of death is so strong, our defenses so well maintained, that when a person receives a terminal diagnosis, he or she is totally unprepared and often hides within a fragile bubble of hope—hope for more time, hope for remission, hope for a breakthrough. Many doctors conspire with their patients well past the time this kind of hope makes sense by not talking about dying. They don't know how to shift the conversation to other, more appropriate forms of hope. They want to avoid the emotional outburst that might accompany an honest assessment of where a patient is in their disease trajectory. Even in the face of obvious disease progression and functional decline, a patient and family will continue to cling to denial. They focus on symptom management, staying positive, and a heroic attempt to keep life "normal."

All of this avoidance in accepting death leads to superficial and blunted interactions between the dying person and their loved ones. Opportunities to explore the meaning of a life go unaddressed. Emotions go unexpressed, wishes unfulfilled. Dying becomes an unrelenting downward spiral of anxiety and exhaustion as families become overwhelmed by the tasks of caregiving and doubt about doing it right. In the emptiness and excruciating sadness that follow a death, a heavy sense of guilt for holding on too long to pretense or secrecy overshadows the grief.

But dying doesn't need to be this bleak, this soul wrenching. A new approach to dying is emerging, one that encourages a dying person and their loved ones to face their fear, break through denial, and engage in an honest, open exploration of death and dying.

This approach also goes well beyond rupturing the thick crust of denial and evasion that separates us from facing death more directly. It also encourages people to explore the meaning of their lives and to express that meaning through memory books, videos, scrolls, or decorated boxes that hold special objects or stories. It helps people to introduce a sense of sacredness into the dying process; to establish how they want the space around them to look and feel in the last days of life. It introduces the idea of designing rituals they can conduct during the last days, which will enrich the meaning of the experience. It teaches the use of guided imagery, touch, and music to bring greater comfort to everyone.

And, finally, it helps family understand the importance of reprocessing the dying experience after their loved one dies, reshaping the images and thoughts that may be haunting their waking mind and their dreams. Naturally, this approach to dying helps the patient and family to be more in control of how the dying process will unfold.

The approach I have just outlined is one that a dying person and the family can learn and incorporate into their experience in many ways. The approach was inspired by the work that birth doulas do with a woman in labor. There is now a growing field of people who guide and support the dying and their families through the labor of death. They are referred to as end-of-life doulas, death doulas, or death midwives. Like their counterparts in birth, death doulas coach a dying person and the family through the entire experience: helping them plan for the last days of life; supporting them emotionally, spiritually, and physically through the labor of dying; then helping family emotionally after the death.

My work as a death doula began in 2003, when I created the first hospice-based end-of-life doula program in the country. At the time, I had been a hospice social worker for only six years. I had entered the field in my late forties, after four years as a hospice volunteer and having returned to graduate school for my social work degree. My exposure to dying people and those in grief made me realize that I felt a calling to this work.

Over and over again as I served dying patients and their families at a large New York City hospice, I saw less-than-ideal deaths: a patient being rushed off to die in the hospital, even though they wanted to die at home; a husband or wife sleeping through the death of their spouse in the next room because they were too exhausted to stay up or didn't recognize the symptoms of imminent death; an adult child not called to the bedside for the last breaths because a paid caregiver took it upon themselves to "protect" that child from the supposed pain of watching the death. I could go on enumerating the ways endings stole meaning and peace of mind from both the dying and their loved ones due to a poor understanding of or preparation for death, even under the enlightened approach of hospice.

As I struggled with observing these unfortunate deaths, I tried to see how I as a social worker could do my job better or help the hospice I worked for find a different way to work with the dying at the very end of their illness. It wasn't that the hospice administration didn't see what I saw. It wasn't that they didn't have the heart to change it. It was just that the structure of hospice and the logistics of caring for so many people spread across the city in their own homes just didn't allow for the kinds of care we all wanted to provide.

During those very early days of 2003, I had a friend who decided to abandon a PhD program in anthropology and become a birth doula instead. She wanted to move from the academic career she had originally envisioned into actively working with people to transform the experience of birth. As she told me what she was learning and how she was working with women in labor, I realized that the birth doula model might also work really well at the end of life. There are so many similarities between birth and death that adapting the approaches and philosophy, even the techniques, of birth doulas to end-of-life work was relatively straightforward. Eventually, I took birth doula training myself, so I could see exactly what they learned and adapt it to working with people going through the labor of dying.

After thoroughly researching the field to see if anyone else was approaching the end of life in this way, I became convinced that I had hit on an approach that no one else had tried. I discussed my idea with the CEO of my hospice and received her blessing to begin an end-of-life doula program. The first class I taught, at the end of 2003, had seventeen people in it. In early 2004, we became the first death doulas in the United States working to guide people through the last days of their life. Since then I have worked with hundreds of people in their dying process and taught close to two thousand people how to do the work of being a death doula professionally or simply to help their friends, families, or communities. The stories I tell in these pages are woven from the fabric of these years of experience.

The fullest expression of the end-of-life doula approach may be embodied in specially trained individuals. But everyone can learn from the principles and techniques of death doulas, transforming their own experience as a dying person or family caregiver. This book is dedicated to helping anyone learn the guiding principles of this new approach to dying and conveying the spirit that animates it through the stories presented. However, to become a death doula who serves dying people outside one's family or circle of friends, it is important to take an appropriate training program. And, even for those people who only imagine using this approach with people they know, formal training can expand their knowledge and bolster their skills.

Beyond exposing you to the doula approach of dealing with death and dying, I hope this book helps you to see that death doesn't need to terrify you. That you can prepare for the end of your life, or the life of someone you love, in a way that deepens the experience and uplifts you at the same time.

CHAPTER 1

A Tale of Two Deaths

"It's not that I'm afraid to die—I just don't want to be there when it happens." This funny and nuanced remark from the book *Without Feathers,* by Woody Allen, sums up what many people feel: it isn't death itself that is so terrifying, it is the process of dying that truly scares people. And for good reason. We have managed in Western society to prolong the dying process. Not in a way that gives us more quality time but in a way that extends our suffering and diminishes our dignity. So, naturally we don't want to be around when we're dying—behind Allen's punch line lies the bitter truth of pain and suffering.

However, it doesn't need to be this way. The following two stories illustrate very different experiences of death. The first tells the unfortunate story of Sam, whose death was typical of the way too many people still die today. The second story is about Sam's wife Gloria, who died only six years later but in a very different way. Her death illustrates a new approach that elevates the experience by deepening meaning and offering a sublime peace in the last days.

Sam was diagnosed with tongue cancer shortly after celebrating his seventieth birthday. He felt something underneath the side of his tongue, as if a piece of food were stuck there or he had a cold sore. But it didn't go away and got progressively worse. Finally, he went to the doctor and after a biopsy was quickly diagnosed.

He fought the disease for more than twelve years. He had chemotherapy and radiation before trying alternative methods, traveling to Germany a number of times. At points, treatments slowed the disease, but eventually the cancer became more aggressive, and no treatment could halt its progression.

Toward the end, Sam allowed the doctor and his wife to convince him to have a tracheotomy because of the way the tumor was growing. After that, he spoke with great difficulty and discomfort, was often misunderstood by people, and could only get food through a tube in his abdomen, which required a lengthy process overnight or awkward sessions during the day. Sam's life narrowed to the most basic tasks of surviving, robbing him of all sense of meaning and joy.

Late one morning, when a privately hired home health aide came to wash and dress Sam, she found him unresponsive. She panicked his wife into calling 911. EMS came and took Sam to the emergency room of the nearest hospital—not one he had been to before. The hospitalist put Sam through a number of tests even as he slipped further into a coma. Late in the evening, the doctor briefly talked with Sam's wife. He told her that the only option now was a risky surgery that might stop the internal bleeding caused by the tumor. After nearly twelve hours of sitting in the overcrowded and uncomfortable emergency room, Sam's wife decided, with the encouragement of the nurses, to go home and get some rest. The nurses suggested that she come back in the morning when the doctor would do the surgery.

In the middle of the night, due to another wave of admissions to the emergency room, a nurse's assistant pushed Sam out into an empty hallway alongside the emergency room. Finally, in the early morning, he was placed in a regular room upstairs with a patient who was in a lot of pain and moaning loudly. When the day nurse came on duty at seven o'clock, she looked in on her new patient and saw that his vital signs were quite weak. She updated Sam's chart, then went on with her other duties.

Sam's wife arrived at the hospital around eight, because the surgery was scheduled for eight thirty that morning, and she wanted to see him before it started. When she pulled back the curtain that separated Sam from the man in the bed by the door, she discovered that he had died.

The last day of Sam's life had been consumed by hours of futile tests, under the care of a doctor who didn't know him or his wife, lying for a time in an empty hallway, then subjected to the moans of an unknown roommate. There wasn't one personal item or picture of Sam's in the room, nor did he have the opportunity to feel and hear the loving presence of his wife or their two children in his last hours. Sam had had the most advanced medical treatment available and died the most alone, sterile kind of death.

Sam's wife Gloria was diagnosed with ovarian cancer only four and a half years after Sam died—almost to the day. Gloria maintained her normal life and activities for close to a year after her diagnosis, living alone in the house that she and Sam had purchased when they had started their family. She did two rounds of chemotherapy, but still the cancer spread. After completing the second round, she decided to stop treatment, remembering how continued treatment had devastated Sam's quality of life.

As her energy level waned, Gloria realized that she needed help. Her daughter took a sabbatical from work and moved in with her. Shortly after that, they requested hospice care. They were fortunate that the local hospice program offered an end-of-life doula service conducted by specially trained volunteers.

After getting to know Gloria and her daughter, the doula who had the primary responsibility of working with them began talking to Gloria about significant events in her life, things she had learned over the years, values she had tried to live by. The doula explained that most people approaching the end of their life very naturally look back to ponder how well they lived and consider the mistakes they may have made. If a person engages actively in these times of reflection, it leads to a process of summing up that can help the person extract meaning from their life's journey.

At first, Gloria didn't know what to make of the talk about summing up and meaning. But she did acknowledge that at moments, when she sat alone on the couch or lay in bed, her mind would be pulled into one memory or another—mostly the important ones that felt good to her, but sometimes even the ones that made her cringe. Suddenly, a smell or a particular color, Sam's face when he looked lovingly at one of their children, and many, many other bits of her life experience would just float to the surface of her mind then disappear. The doula encouraged these reminiscences as one way of starting to uncover the deeper layers of meaning in her life.

At some point, Gloria remembered the shoe boxes filled with cards Sam had given her on every anniversary, birthday, Mother's Day, and Valentine's day. She had her daughter get them from the closet, and they read them together, along with the cards Gloria had given Sam on all those same occasions. It took many days to read them all. They had a profound effect on Gloria and her daughter. So much so, that the doula recommended they build a legacy project out of them.

A legacy project is a way to capture and express an important aspect of a person's life. It gives that person an opportunity to explore and appreciate that part of their life in a deep way that can be very satisfying, even transformative. It also gives family a way to hold on to that person after they die—remembering the imprint of that person's life on their lives. For future generations, it is a way to appreciate who this ancestor was and what was important to them.

With the help of the doula, Gloria, her two children, and her oldest grandchild created two large collages—one for the family of each of her children—that incorporated images and words from many of the greeting cards. The collages were visually stunning and captured forever the words of love that Gloria and Sam had exchanged from the time they had started dating right up to Sam's death. But the best part of this legacy work was the opportunity that Gloria had to speak to her two children directly about the important values that had sustained and deepened her relationship with Sam over the years. The collages would act as reminders of the precious time Gloria, her children, and grandchild spent together working on them, as much as the values the collages expressed.

One of the most important realizations that came out of this work was that Gloria's legacy was intimately interconnected to Sam's legacy. So, although Sam didn't have the same opportunity to look back over his life, in a sense Gloria and her children had done it for him through Gloria's legacy project. Even though it was years after his death, the collages brought greater balance to some of the negative memories of his dying experience.

During the visits to work on the legacy project, the doula also introduced the technique of guided imagery, which, she explained, could help Gloria feel a greater sense of well-being or help moderate the severity of a symptom. The doula built a guided imagery session around Gloria's description of a beach she loved on Martha's Vineyard, one that she and Sam had taken their children to for a number of summers. The doula and the family also discussed how to bring a sense of the sacred into the space where Gloria would die and a ritual they would do right after she took her last breath.

Six months after Gloria's daughter had moved in, Gloria's body started the final process of breaking down. Gloria remained at home, as she had requested, surrounded by photographs of her family, friends, and trips she and Sam had taken. Lavender candles burned through the night, the soft glow of their flames filling the air with her favorite scent. Now the doulas came in shifts around the clock, being at Gloria's bedside with her children, friends, and other members of the family. The doulas made sure that Gloria's lips and mouth stayed moist, held her hand, caressed her face and head, spoke of the beach through the woods on Martha's Vineyard, and played the James Taylor CDs she loved so much. From time to time, the doulas, a family member, or a friend would read a greeting card randomly from those mounted on the legacy boards or selected from those still sitting in one of the shoe boxes kept near the bed.

The doulas provided emotional and spiritual support to Gloria's children and grandchild as well. One doula encouraged Gloria's daughter to get in bed and spend an hour or two snuggling up to her mother and caressing her face and arm. Another encouraged Gloria's son to tell his favorite stories about his mother and his father, and hugged him when he cried. The doulas reminded the family that hearing was the last of the senses to go, so they would continue to tell her how much they loved her, how much they had learned from her, and that it was okay for her to let go of her body whenever she was ready.

After nearly three days of shifts, the doula who was there during the middle of the night recognized that Gloria was quite close to the end. She woke Gloria's daughter and called Gloria's son so he could come from the next town to be at the bedside. When Gloria took her last soft, shallow breaths—about an hour and a half later—everyone was there with her.

As had been decided months earlier, in discussion with the doula, Gloria's daughter washed her mother's body with warm, lavender-scented water. With Gloria's body covered, her son washed her hair and combed it out. The doula helped the daughter clothe Gloria in the outfit she had selected for herself. Then everyone gathered around the bed, held hands, and observed a time of silence. As part of this ritual of closure, Gloria had asked that everyone present say whatever was in his or her heart at the time.

Then the doula opened and read a greeting card that Gloria had written for this moment. Gloria asked that each person connect to the love that was in their hearts, which began with the love she and Sam had offered them unconditionally every day of their lives. Love that bonded their two children together and the love for those they had brought into the family. Love, she said, was the most important gift anyone could offer or receive—it was the deepest truth she could share with them.

Gloria's dying experience was the antithesis in many ways of the experience Sam had suffered through. What made it so different was the exposure to ideas that deepened the experience and allowed Gloria to orchestrate how she wanted the end of her life to unfold. While the doulas acted as the catalyst in this process, opening the door to a different way to approach death, it was how the family embraced this approach and ran with it that really made all the difference.

These two tales of death show clearly the difference between a process that rests on medical intervention, evasion, and fear and one based on an open-eyed engagement with the dying process, a focus on legacy, and loving presence. The kind of death Gloria had is the kind of death you or a loved one can have by bringing the doula principles and techniques into the experience. It's all about opening to this new way of dying and creatively adapting what you will read in the following pages to your situation. And, if you feel a calling to serve others during their journey toward death, you will find here what you need to get started down that path.

CHAPTER 2

The End-of-Life Doula Approach

Dying from a terminal illness takes months, often years. As a dying person's functional ability declines, the demands on caregivers increase. So, by the time the dying person's body starts its final process of breaking down, the family is likely to be exhausted emotionally and physically. Yet, at this point, family feels called on to be even more present, because they recognize the end is near. They could use increased support, but professional medical help is only sporadically available—and often not there in the critical moments, when a new symptom appears or one worsens in a way the family wasn't prepared for.

If the dying person is at home on hospice care, a nurse, social worker, or chaplain will call at a crisis moment and even try to visit. But, due to the number of other patients they serve and the time it takes to get from one location to another, they often can't respond quickly enough or actually get there when it matters most. The structure and logistics of hospice care just don't allow for the best care at the very end of life.

The same is true if a person is dying in a hospital or other facility. While professionals may have easier access to a dying person—because they don't have to travel to get from one patient to another—they are still limited by their shift schedules and the number of other patients they have to serve. On weekends and at night, when there are far fewer staff members, the problem gets even worse.

So, for the last hours to days of life, a dying person and the family may feel the full weight of the dying process on their shoulders and have minimal assistance. They can feel abandoned, alone, and ill-prepared. Their focus narrows to basic physical care, they stuff down their emotions as best they can, and they move through the experience in a disconnected daze. I have seen this over and over again in the families of dying people, and I experienced it in my own family when my father was actively dying fifteen years ago.

Even though my mother had hired an aide to help with my dad's care in the last couple of months, she was hardly sleeping at night and on edge during the day as she saw to all my dad's needs. My dad was ninety years old, and my mom was seventy-seven at the time. Until the last week or so, she maintained the household and went to work every day, managing a forty-story commercial building in the middle of Manhattan. My sister lived across town and helped out many days during the week. I lived an hour and a half away, so I could only get down once a week or, on occasion, two times in a week.

On the days I could be there during the last few weeks, I slept in a bed right next to my dad. I made my mom sleep on the couch in the living room, so she wouldn't be disturbed during the night by every sound my father made or his slightest movement. But even with all this help, my mother was beyond exhausted.

Although my father went through his dying process years before I formulated the end-of-life doula approach, I was at that time a hospice social worker. Still, we as a family cared for my father and lived our daily lives behind a heavy drape of denial that kept out the truth of his dying. For a time, my sister clung to the idea that a new pinpoint radiation technology might cure him. For a long time, we all held on to the belief that we might hold death at bay and have more time with him. There were times when his decline seemed to pause. Although his functional deterioration was profound, in those times he seemed to hold his own against further descent toward death—and we would believe in our denial again. But then the process would continue, and the truth of his dying would break through our denial.

Four days before he died, we knew that death was close. He had stopped eating weeks earlier. Now he was "sleeping" all the time. It was painfully obvious that his body had entered the final process of breaking down; all his systems were failing.

In those last days, my father's dying process weighed on all of us considerably. We didn't talk much about the feelings we were experiencing, but I could see it on my mother's and sister's faces, and I'm sure they could see it on mine. At least I knew enough about the process to inform my mother and sister about some of the signs and symptoms we witnessed. But I also remember wishing that a dispassionate outsider, one with more knowledge than I had, could be there to help us read the signs more clearly and to support us emotionally. Of course we supported each other the best we could, but it wasn't really enough. I remember feeling very alone. And, during the last several days, I don't remember the hospice nurse coming more than once—and then only for perhaps an hour.

I spent the entire night before my father died in the bed next to him. I remember that a lamp on the night table cast a pale yellow light across half the bed, leaving the rest of the room mostly dark. My father was a little restless, and the slightest movement or sound he made kept me from falling asleep. I didn't know that night how close he was to dying, but it was clear that his death wasn't far off, and thoughts of what life would be like without him kept swirling around in my head. All my life, my dad had been a gentle, sweet presence. Somehow I couldn't imagine the world without him.

At 6:00 a.m. I left to go back home. It was a Thursday, and there was an event in my older son's class that morning that I wanted to attend. But as soon as I arrived home, my wife told me that my mom had called to say that I should go back because my dad had taken a sudden turn for the worse. I kissed my kids and left without even washing my face or brushing my teeth.

When I reentered my father's bedroom I saw that his limbs looked very stiff, and he didn't move at all. The only motion in his body was the shallow rise and fall of his chest as he breathed—and each time he exhaled, his chest remained motionless for a long pause before the next inhalation.

I settled into watching him, perched on the side of the twin bed just a foot from where he lay. For the next three hours his breath continued to slow, with longer and longer periods of apnea. In the late morning, the aide arrived and came to sit in the bedroom as well. My mother and sister came in at points and spent time sitting near him. Finally, my legs and back stiff from sitting, I decided to walk to the kitchen to stretch and get a drink of water. My sister and the aide were sitting off to the side near the windows, talking to each other. I was out of the room for at most three minutes.

As I stepped back into the bedroom, I saw that my father wasn't breathing. I stopped in the entrance to the room, frozen by his stillness, waiting to see if the next in-breath would come before I went back to sitting at his bedside. After a minute of waiting, I realized that he wasn't going to breathe again. My sister and the aide, who hadn't been looking over at my dad, realized that I wasn't coming farther into the room and asked me if he was gone. By now almost another minute had passed.

"I think so," I said, then went to get my mom. We all huddled together on one side of the bed, holding each other and watching for several more minutes before we called the hospice nurse to let her know that my father had died. The nurse hadn't visited him for the past three days.

Looking back, I don't remember immediately feeling guilty about going to the kitchen and missing his last breath. My father had never talked about wanting us to be with him when he died.

In fact, knowing my father, he would have only wanted his death to be as easy as possible for all of us. He would have said we should do whatever was best for us. But, as the fact that he had actually died became more real and we made preparations for his funeral, that feeling of guilt wormed its way into my thoughts, and I realized that unconsciously this had been important to me.

He was buried three days later, on a Sunday, with swirling flakes of snow like bits of paper falling from the sky. It was bitter cold for early April, chilling us as we stood around his open grave. I remember my wife clutching me as we huddled together with my mother and sister. The rabbi read prayers I didn't understand, yet their rhythmic, melancholy sound was so familiar. There is something in Jewish prayer that always sounds to me like a cry from the heart, a cry of deep, unfulfilled yearning. I could feel that cry in my heart as I watched the flecks of snow starting to coat the top of the huge pile of orange-brown dirt at the side of the grave. I stopped hearing the prayers and turned inward, silently apologizing to my father for not staying next to him and holding his hand as he took his last breath.

In the days that followed, I found myself apologizing over and over again but not being able to let go of the guilt. When those thoughts came up, I would berate myself for going to the kitchen at just the time when he was dying. It felt as if I had abandoned him just as he needed someone who loved him to be at his side.

Many months later, I finally arrived at a rationale that began to ease my guilt. I started to weigh those last moments of not being there against all the hours of caring for him in the seven months of his illness. I added into that equation the many times I had told him I loved and admired him.

Even though I came to accept that my not being present for my father's last breath was okay, I still would rather have been present. In the years that followed my father's death, I came to know the dying process a lot better. Now I can read the signs of imminent death. If my father were dying today, I would not leave his bedside when those signs were present. And now I teach those signs to other people so they won't have to struggle with months of guilt as I did.

Not being present at the end of a loved one's life is only one way a death can cause unnecessary anguish. Sometimes people end up going to the hospital, even though they didn't want to die there; sometimes relationships that could be healed, or at least improved, are left hanging, because death is never discussed; sometimes the spiritual distress of the person dying goes unrecognized or unattended. All these failures, and many others, result in deaths with extra layers of suffering that could have been avoided.

It isn't just the negative events and circumstances that make many deaths so unfortunate; there are missed opportunities for deeper meaning and greater comfort that most people don't even realize can be part of the experience. Over the last one hundred or more years, as a result of the rise in hospitals and health-care technology, death and dying have become highly medicalized. There have been a number of regrettable side effects from this development. For one thing, people don't attend to the internal impulse to explore the meaning of their life. For another, advances in technology and medicines extend life in a state of dramatically diminished quality, which only increases physical and emotional suffering for the dying person—and, by extension, for the family.

As a hospice social worker, I encountered these negative aspects of dying every day. They are what propelled me to contemplate a different approach to death and dying, which resulted in my formulating the end-of-life doula approach with its emphases on meaning, legacy work, planning, attention to the sacred nature of dying, alternative interventions for symptom management, intense involvement in the last days of life, reprocessing the experiences with loved ones after the death, and, finally, active involvement in early grief. This model has stayed fundamentally the same over the last thirteen years. Nonetheless, some aspects of it have evolved and become much more important as the movement it spawned has grown. I expect that it will continue to evolve as other developments in the field of death and dying are incorporated into the model.

The end-of-life doula approach encompasses three different areas of activity. The first of these involves the dying person reflecting on their life and planning for how they envision the last days of life to unfold. The second area centers on holding the space for the plan of those last days, when the body is finally breaking down. The last part of the program begins shortly after the person dies, as family and friends process their experiences of the dying time and begin their work on grief.

Reflection

According to developmental psychologist Erik Erickson, the impulse to reflect on one's life is an inborn imperative that naturally occurs as a person reaches the last stage of life: old age. Erickson saw different chronological periods of life presenting developmental challenges that led to either greater personality wholeness and a sense of well-being or poorer adaptation to the world and a contracted sense of self. He named each developmental stage with the words that defined the crisis at the center of its psychosocial challenge. He called the last stage of the lifespan "Ego Integrity vs. Despair." At the heart of the conflict between ego integrity and despair are two questions: "Has my life had meaning?" and "Has my life been satisfying?" How a person answers these questions leads in the direction of either ego integrity or despair.

As a person faces a terminal diagnosis, I believe that they are automatically plunged into Erikson's final developmental stage—no matter how old they happen to be at the time. I have seen dying people in their late twenties and earlier thirties wrestle with these questions as actively as people in their eighties and nineties.

If a dying person is able to attain ego integrity in the process of reflecting on their life, they come to feel proud of their accomplishments, understand the meaning contained in their life, and achieve a positive sense of completion. Further, they recognize the legacies they will leave behind. If a person fails at this developmental challenge, then they end up believing that their life was wasted; they settle into feelings of regret, bitterness, and despair.

The path to engaging the questions at the heart of this developmental stage involves introspection, journaling, reminiscence, life review, and, at times, deep exploration with other people. To do this work in a meaningful way, the person needs to approach it with a serious, structured examination. They have to look at both the accomplishments and things learned over the course of their life, as well as the failures, discarded beliefs, and unfinished business.

As the process unfolds, the dying person will naturally review the most important events in their life. They will examine how they felt about those events at the time, how they understand the impact of those events on their life, and what if anything they still may need to do in response to those events. Other areas of exploration involve themes that a person sees woven across the fabric of their experience, values that have become important to them, and things they learned—from either success or failure. All of this is fertile ground for understanding a person's life.

The exploration into meaning can happen in dialog with a doula or family member; in moments of inner reflection, when the dying person is alone; in the effort to crystallize the meaning into a concrete legacy that can be passed on to others; and in discussion with family and friends, who can contribute a perspective the dying person may not fully recognize.

Too often, this work of exploring meaning is left undone. If the dying person and the family are not openly discussing dying, or they are trying to maintain an air of normalcy, then reminiscence or life review tends to happen only in fleeting moments when the dying person is alone. Real examination of a person's life needs structure to arrive at meaning. Without structure, despair is too often the outcome.

As a person explores the meaning of their life, it is natural to consider how that meaning might be expressed in a concrete way that the person finds satisfying; in a way that loved ones will find informative or inspiring. This expression of meaning is referred to as a legacy project. It can take the form of a memory book or an illustrated box that contains objects and/or cards with messages from family and friends. It can be an audio or video interview that focuses in a deep way on one or more aspects of a person's life. It can be a life scroll that illustrates important moments or recurring themes. Or it might be a series of letters to current or future family members, expressing thoughts and wishes for them when they reach important milestones in their lives. The kinds of legacy projects people create are limited only by the imagination and creativity of those involved. Over time, these legacies become deeply valued family treasures, because they allow people to reconnect with the person after they have died and reengage with the meaning they identified.

A legacy project does more than express meaning. It preserves personal and, therefore, family history. It also gives a dying person the opportunity to exercise more control over how they spend their time in the last months or weeks of life. Loss of control over many aspects of life is a common complaint in severe illness and approaching death. Any way you can return some measure of control is therefore very helpful to the emotional state of the dying person and improves the quality of their life.

Too often, a dying person is treated as if they have already died. Their opinions, ideas, or advice about family events or issues is no longer solicited; they are left out of everyday decisions or ones that involve planning for the future. Creating a legacy project gives back to a dying person the power of who they are and returns their relevance to those around them. After they die, the legacy continues to speak for them, to tell their story, express their values, to convey their hopes for those who survive them or who may be born long afterward.

Planning

Living with a terminal illness means facing not only the loss of one's life but also the progressive loss of identity, autonomy, functional ability, and control. As these losses pile up, the dying person feels more and more diminished. Too often, family and friends, even professional caregivers, pay little attention to these losses and the devastating impact they have on the emotional and psychological well-being of the person dying.

Working on meaning and legacy can certainly help to reverse some of this impact, as it gives the dying person a sense of purpose and more control over how they live through their dying process. Another approach that can return a sense of autonomy and control is to work on planning for the last days of life. When a dying person reaches that point in their illness, they will no longer be able to speak for themselves or make decisions about how care is delivered. That is why thinking about these choices earlier and making "vigil plans" are so important.

The dying person should consider their choices in regard to medical interventions, the nature of the space and atmosphere around their bedside, and the kinds of interactions with caregivers and visitors they want. Planning for what a person wants in these areas can also make the dying experience more meaningful for the family and bring greater comfort to everyone involved.

One of the primary choices a dying person has is where they will die. For most people, that choice is home. It is the place where we get to be ourselves the most completely; the place where we feel protected, safe, and comfortable. Home is the place where we display reminders of journeys, photos of those we love, objects that we find uplifting for their beauty or their symbolic connection to our beliefs. It is where we raised our children, made love, cried and screamed at losses, entertained, observed the passage of time, dreamed, and took care of ourselves and those close to us. Many of the best memories of our life have soaked into the space, like a fine, almost imperceptible patina that coats every surface and gives it an emotional luster that is particular to the lives that have lived there.

Sometimes dying at home isn't acceptable or possible. Certain cultures believe that death shouldn't occur where people live so that the dead person's spirit will not have difficulty leaving those they loved. Sometimes symptoms can't be well managed at home and need the closeness of nurses and doctors around the clock. Sometimes caregivers are so debilitated by all the care they have given for months, if not years, that they reach a point at which they can't go on—either temporarily or permanently.

Under these conditions, the dying person may be moved to a hospice in-patient unit, a nursing home, or even the hospital, so the caregivers can feel comfortable or have respite.

If the dying person needs to spend the last days of life outside their home, then it is important to consider how the more sterile and institutional space of a hospital or facility room can be made to feel more like home. Not in a generic sense by using more homey furnishings, more colorful walls, or pleasant curtains over the window; but by bringing into the space the person's own photos, art, and objects so that the space becomes theirs and reflects what is most important to them.

Even if a person is dying at home, they may not be in their bedroom. At times, the family room or living room allows the dying person to remain more in the center of family activity, keeps them from having to negotiate steps or longer distances to the bathroom, and may allow them to see the outdoors more easily. Whatever room the person is dying in should have the objects that matter to them the most. This may mean taking photos, art, or religious objects from other rooms and placing them around the bed or on the walls. It may mean rearranging furniture to make viewing things easier or to change the feel of the room.

Then there are a host of other choices about the space that one should consider. What is the light like in the room—day and night? Does the person want strong natural light, shaded light, soft honey-colored light from standing lamps at night, strands of tiny blue or white lights strung along the ceiling molding? And what about candles—the kind you light with a match or are battery operated?

Sound is another important consideration. Does the person want jazz, new age, or classical music; perhaps nature sounds, train whistles in the distance, or live singing. They should also consider the smells in the space: anything from the smell of roses to lavender-scented diffusers, sandalwood incense, orange-scented candles, or the natural smell of the earth and trees through an open window.

Beyond how the space looks, sounds, smells, and feels, a dying person has choices to make about medical interventions and how they want to interact with the people involved in their care and those who visit them. Typically, in the last months of life, and particularly in the last weeks, a dying person experiences symptoms that doctors and nurses medicate, often without asking if the person agrees with that approach. Medical interventions should always be presented with the pros and cons of those interventions. But when it comes to treatment of symptoms, a patient is often told: "I'm going to give you this, which will help with this symptom." The side effects of the medications, not to mention their impact on overall quality of life, are frequently not discussed in a thorough way.

In terminal illness, pain is one of the most frequent symptoms. The severity of pain varies depending on the illness and many other factors that relate to a particular person's physiology and situation. We know that pain is only partly physical—the rest is psychological, emotional, and spiritual. So medication alone should not be relied on to treat pain at end of life. Doctors and nurses often view pain as primarily a medical issue, and they may prescribe an opioid without assessing the other factors contributing to the pain. Even though opioids are generally well tolerated, and side effects can usually be well addressed with other medications, their pros and cons often are not presented. Any time a medication is suggested or the dosage increased, there should be a full assessment and discussion about the rationale, the nature of the expected benefit, the downside, and upcoming life events or circumstances that might be affected by the choice.

We have been taught by countless interactions with medical personnel over our lifetime to rely on the doctor and nurse to do what is right based on their expert knowledge. But this conditioned response doesn't serve us well in understanding the real choices we have. And what we don't realize is that often doctors and nurses speak with an assurance that belies the underlying guesswork of their recommendations.

The mechanism for many medicines is still poorly understood, and the actual response that a particular person will have to a medication can be surprising. Medicine still has an awful lot of experimentation and artistry mixed in with the science. All this is to say that people should ask doctors and nurses a lot more so that they may understand the benefits and impacts of the medicines and interventions that have been suggested before agreeing to their use. This is true for any medication used to treat the symptoms of anxiety, restlessness, secretions (a buildup of liquids in the airways), nausea, vomiting, and so on.

A dying person at home should also be offered the choice of using a hospital bed or staying in their own bed. The bed a person sleeps in is often important to them. A hospital bed may make it easier to provide physical care, but using pillows to prop a person in various ways can also be effective. Some other care choices relate to the use of a Foley catheter, incontinence undergarments, and repositioning the person's body during the last days of life. These decisions have to do with a person's level of comfort, sense of dignity, and their belief about disturbing the natural process of dying. As a dying person grows weaker, and their cognitive ability is more compromised, it is helpful for someone to advocate for the choices the dying person has already made. Since an end-of-life doula isn't emotionally involved in these decisions, they can advocate well, using the vigil plan as a guide.

Alternative methods of dealing with symptoms are also available and can complement the more traditional approaches and medications. Alternatives, such as acupuncture, Reiki, aromatherapy, or lymphatic massage, should be performed only by practitioners with recognized credentials. But guided imagery, another alternative technique, can be effectively used with limited training. Even a dying person can be easily taught how to use this technique for themselves. Guided imagery uses a person's imagination to have a physical, emotional, or even spiritual impact. It can be used for better symptom management, helping a person to feel a general sense of well-being, or to achieve a deeper connection to their spiritual life.

Self-guided imagery or guiding another person takes some practice, but even a person without any experience at all can do an okay job if they go inward and visualize what they are guiding the other person to see, hear, smell, and feel. Chapter 9 is devoted to guided imagery and how to do it well.

A key area of planning for the last days deals with the kinds of interactions the dying person wants to have with family, friends, and caregivers. For some people, the thought of family and friends holding their hand as they sit at the bedside, caressing their face, or even climbing in bed to lie beside and against them makes them feel loved and brings a sense of reassurance. Other people may want to limit the amount of touch, because they feel that it may distract them from their internal process of dying or pull them back to involvement with a world they must leave behind.

Even for those people who want physical involvement, they may want only certain kinds of touch, and then only where it feels good. I have known a number of people who find it unacceptable for anyone but their husband or wife to massage or caress their feet. In the same way, some people like the idea of a family member or a doula holding their hand or caressing their arm, but they don't want people caressing their face or climbing in bed to snuggle up with them—that is too intimate unless it is a close family member.

Since doulas are not family, they may have an easier time advocating for what the dying person wants with family and friends who may not understand or have not imagined that their loved one would make such requests. The doula may also need to model how to touch the dying person or instruct family and friends on how to best hold the person to create feelings of safety and comfort.

In addition to physical touch, the dying person should decide what kind of verbal interaction they want with those who will sit at their bedside. Do they want stories of the times they spent together, words of love and reassurance, prayer, silent meditation, confessions and forgiveness, reading from the Bible or books of poetry, the news of the day? They may want young children at the bedside—as long as the children are comfortable being there—or they may not want the turmoil that children could bring to the space in which they are dying.

The discussions about choices and wishes lead to a plan for the last days that will be written down so that the family has a document to remind them and others who visit what their loved one wants. The plan also serves as guide for doulas who may work in shifts around the clock to support the dying person and the family in the last days of life. It is a formal acknowledgment of a person's right to spend the last days of their life in a way that honors them. It's the script for what a "good death" means to them: how they envision those last days will look, sound, and feel.

This is not to say, of course, that the last days of life will turn out exactly as scripted. Sometimes things that seemed right during planning don't work well during the vigil. Sometimes things that weren't discussed at all come up and offer opportunities that can change for the better the feeling in the space or the involvement with loved ones. Again, because the doula is not a family member and doesn't have that kind of emotional connection, they may be capable of observing things the family can't.

For example, I once went to see how the vigil was going for a matriarch in an Italian family. She was in a basement apartment of her single-family house. The apartment was one large room with the bed in a corner, an open kitchen at the other end, and a family space between them.

Day or night, family filled the room: the woman's sister and her husband, her two daughters, a son, their spouses and their children in their twenties and teens, cousins who were as close as children, nieces and nephews, and neighbors who lived alongside them for forty or more years. During my visit, two or three people sat at the bedside at all times. The woman's husband sat at the head of the bed on one side most of the time, looking shell-shocked. He held his wife's hand as if it were made of wood. Family would come over and talk with him briefly, but he would only look down at his wife's fingers in his hand, occasionally rubbing his thumb across them as if he could encourage more life back into them.

At one point, as I stood with the doula talking about the vigil, she leaned in to me to say quietly, "He looks so cut off; I think all the people inhibit his interaction with his wife. I wonder if there are things he needs to say to her but can't with all these people around constantly." I suggested the doula talk to one of his daughters about her observation.

When the daughter heard what the doula was seeing, she immediately realized the truth of it, even though she hadn't seen it for herself prior to the doula mentioning it. She went right over to her father to see if he wanted time alone with his dying wife. He did. So the daughter and the doula ushered everyone upstairs to a living room they hadn't used in over a year. We sat in awkward silence punctuated occasionally by whispered exchanges.

The only other noises in the room came from people shifting position on the stiff plastic covering the chairs and couch.

After about twenty minutes, the daughter who had helped lead us upstairs went to check on her father. She came back to report that he was ready for everyone to return to the apartment. We all trooped back downstairs. Later, this daughter told me that those twenty minutes her father had alone with her mother were the best thing that happened during the vigil. "It would never have happened if your doula hadn't suggested it to me—I just didn't see what my father needed."

The reflection and planning work can take weeks to months of effort, depending on how deeply involved the dying person and the family get. While the ideal is to spend as much time as needed, disease progression can overwhelm this process, forcing people to dramatically compress the work. And, sometimes, people don't get to do the summing up and planning work at all prior to the time the person starts actively dying. In that case, it is best to do a simplified version of work on meaning, a legacy, and a plan in the early part of the vigil, while still focusing mostly on emotional and spiritual support. At a minimum, if there is some degree of planning that is accomplished, then at least there will be a blueprint to follow for conducting the remainder of the vigil.

The Vigil

A vigil begins when it is clear that the person is in the final stage of their dying process; that is, when the signs and symptoms suggest that the body is breaking down irrevocably. At this point, it is important for someone to be present at or near the bedside around the clock—unless the dying person has specifically asked to be alone during certain times in their process. A vigil can stretch on for days, sometimes even longer than a week, so it is helpful for family and the doulas to stay at the bedside in shifts.

Throughout the vigil, doulas hold the space for the plan the dying person and the family have formulated. Doing that requires a deep engagement with the dying person—even though they may be unresponsive—and with the family. Although the body knows how to die, following a script written into the genes, each death is particular and individual. So the doula and the family must stay alert to what is happening moment by moment.

Each vigil establishes its own rhythm, depending on the speed of decline and the dynamics of the family. The doula synchronizes their activities with this rhythm, intuiting when a particular intervention makes sense. Usually, the doula will determine when it is the right time to use guided visualization, put on music, read something meaningful, or simply caress the arm or face. The series of actions taken often has the quality of a slow dance.

At times, the needs of a family member take precedence over the needs of the dying person, particularly with feelings stirred up by the sights and sounds of the dying process. Family members can rely on the doula to assess when they might need comforting. A doula may hold a hand or give a hug, will know when to reassure a family member with an explanation of symptoms or when to redirect by suggesting they tell a story about the dying person.

The doula walks alongside the family, opening their heart in service and compassion. Doulas do not judge feelings, responses, or behavior. Instead, by their actions and words, doulas convey their support, normalize feelings, model behavior, or gently guide family into a deeper exploration of something they are struggling with. As a result, and in ways that are often mysterious, the doula opens the door to moments of understanding, appreciation, healing, and even transformation.

Two important goals of the doula during the vigil are to provide respite for the family, so they can be more present for the dying person when they aren't resting, and to make sure that the person doesn't die alone. By understanding the signs and symptoms of imminent death, the doula will make sure that the people who should be present for the last breaths are present. By helping the family recognize these signs, the doula prepares them emotionally for the moment when the breath stops.

During the vigil, the doula will assist family or paid caregivers with basic physical care. For the most part, that means making sure the person's mouth and lips stay moist, wiping away any drool, and applying a cool compress if the dying person spikes a fever. The doula will also assist in repositioning a person or changing bedsheets while the person is still lying in the bed. There really isn't a great deal of physical care required when someone is actively dying.

Vigils move inexorably toward the last breath. Time slows and seems to expand; emotions can intensify. Those involved can feel the presence of something momentous filling the space.

Right after the person dies, the doula and the family may conduct a ritual that had been worked out earlier or one that is decided in the spur of the moment. Rituals help people mark a transition from one reality to another in a ceremonial way. Ritual brings order—even if just for a brief time—to the chaos of loss. It helps people accept the reality of death and its place in the life cycle. It gives people the first opportunity to express a sense of loss, and it helps them to celebrate the life that was and that life's impact on their life.

Rituals may come, wholly or in part, directly out of one's traditions and culture. When they do, it connects people to their community and an ancestral experience of loss that may stretch back across time. But rituals can also be designed in a way that incorporates elements from other cultures and traditions and may include elements invented out of personal experience. When rituals are woven together by the dying person and the family, they become expressions of their personality and their particular understanding of death and dying. In my experience, these individualized rituals are very rich in meaning and bring great comfort to those involved.

I once saw an episode of *Hawaii Five-0* on TV that had a ceremony I thought was very moving. To honor a friend who had died, a group of perhaps thirty people went out to the ocean on surfboards. Forming a large circle, they sat astride their boards as one person paddled into the middle of the circle to release their friend's ashes. Then each person removed a lei from around their neck and threw it into the circle as well. Perhaps they spoke or sang, I don't remember. But I was very touched by these few minutes of a ceremony that must have its roots in the native Hawaiian tradition.

Months later, I spoke of this ritual to a dying person and the family. They were moved just hearing about it and wished they could use it in some way. As we discussed it further, we came up with ways to adapt that ritual into one that would capture its spirit but still be possible in the family room where their loved one was dying in a hospital bed.

We decided that after the death, we would move the bed—as best we could—to the center of the room. We planned to include the element of water by filling a bowl with water from a stream behind the house and placing it on a small table at the foot of the bed. Rose petals placed in the water would represent the leis. As we discussed these elements, they took on new meaning for the family. The water in the bowl came to represent the flow of time and the tears of grief. The rose petals torn from the flower came to represent the visceral feeling of loss and an acknowledgment that life is impermanent.

During the ceremony, each person would take a flower petal from the bowl of water and place it on a part of the deceased's body, saying something that celebrated the blessings that person had brought into their life. When that was done, everyone would gather around the bed holding hands and sing a favorite song, followed by a prayer, and ending with a period of silence. After the formal part of the ritual ended, the family decided they would still sit around the bed and tell stories about their loved one. If they felt moved to, they could still go over to the bowl, take a rose petal, and place it on the body.

I have told the story of this ritual to other dying people and their families as an illustration of what is possible and how beautiful and meaningful ritual can be right after someone dies. Other people have adapted parts of this ritual to create their own, adding elements that come from different traditions.

More than one hundred years ago, when it was common for death to occur at home, the body would stay in the home for a day or more so people could gather and view it before everyone marched together to the cemetery to bury the person. Having the body there in the home for a while allowed the family to make its initial adjustment to the death.

Today, in our culture, we try to remove the body as quickly as possible. It is a continuation of our avoidance of death, wanting death removed from our sight. Families can still choose to have the body removed quickly, if that makes sense to them. But letting families know they can take all the time they want, and even keep the body for a home viewing and funeral, gives people the opportunity to participate in every aspect of death.

After a ritual, a doula will stay with the family for as long as they want. The doula might make initial phone calls to the funeral home and friends if the family is too emotional to do that themselves. The doula usually stays through the removal of the body and may wait after that until a particular family member or friend arrives.

Reprocessing

Three to six weeks after the death, one or more of the doulas will meet with family a number of times to help them reprocess the dying experience and begin the early work of grief. The timing of this aspect of doula work is quite intentional. Right after a death, family tend to be very supportive, perhaps staying for days or even a week with those mourning. Friends and neighbors tend to be very attentive, bringing over food, calling, and visiting often.

But after several weeks, the extra attention starts to evaporate. People return to their lives, paying less attention to those who are grieving. That is when the vacuum left by the death starts to really be felt and grief takes hold, which is why this is the time to start reprocessing the death.

As the family tells the story of what they saw, heard, and did, it is possible to detect the things that keep coming back into their minds—especially those connected to negative emotions. The look of their loved one's face at the end—wasted, stiff, and unfamiliar; the gurgling sound of secretions at the bottom of the throat or in the chest; rapid, labored breathing that made it seem as if they were working very hard to get air into their lungs; something hurtful a family member blurted out at the person dying in a moment of exhaustion, frustration, or fear. Just talking about these images or events that haunt their thoughts can relieve some of the distress. It may also be possible to find ways of reframing those experiences to lessen the emotional impact.

During the reprocessing sessions, people also share beautiful or moving moments they have experienced. I carry many of these moments from the vigils I have attended. For example, I well remember the young woman who fought past her fear of being in the room with her dying grandfather. She spent the last three hours of his life half lying on the bed, so her head was on his pillow up against him, as she caressed his head of hair the color of new snow.

Or the wife who held her husband's face tenderly between her hands, leaning over him to tell him how much she loved him. He hadn't spoken for close to a week, but at that moment he breathed the words, "I love you, too." These were the last words he uttered before he died.

Or the image of young teenage girls holding hands with their mother across the bed as their father took his last breaths. Their shining faces, streaked with tears, showed such strength and determination as their mother told them how courageous they had been throughout his illness. She also reassured them that their father would always be in their hearts.

Sharing moments like these gives people positive memories to carry into their grief process, helping to counterbalance some of the more negative images they struggle to shake. I have often heard from people that they used an uplifting memory to very consciously replace a painful memory after it popped into their mind.

The reprocessing experience is very different from telling the story to a grief counselor or in a bereavement group. The doulas contribute an outside, but engaged, perspective that helps the family recapture or discover moments that would have been lost to them otherwise. Since the doulas walk alongside them in the dying experience, telling the story to and with them is so much more powerful.

Sometimes the reprocessing experience may include continued work on a legacy project that had been begun earlier. A legacy project might even be started in the reprocessing visits and extend well into the time of grieving. When children were very actively involved in the dying experience, parents can stay in touch with their grief by having the children work with them on a legacy project. This also provides opportunities to give the children support with their emotions.

Another part of the reprocessing sessions is an introduction to the work of grieving. At a minimum, the doulas can provide an overview of the terrain people will traverse and what they will need to do to recover well. But they may also facilitate the early grief work through a series of visits. Those visits provide opportunities for family members to continue talking about their loved one and the dying process. During this time, the doulas use some of the same principles and techniques that guided the early work on meaning and legacy, as well as the work during the vigil.

For example, guided imagery can be used to replace unwelcome memories, to balance some of the negative emotions with more positive ones, or to work on unfinished business with the person who died. Work on meaning can help someone in grief to rebuild their sense of self or discover a new sense of purpose in their life.

At some point, the doula process needs to end. One way to acknowledge this moment is through a closing ritual. The ritual may have been discussed and created during the planning time or in the early reprocessing visits. The ritual doesn't have to be complex. It can be as simple as lighting a candle, offering words of inspiration, reciting a prayer, or offering a written summation of the dying experience through the eyes of the doulas. Sometimes, doulas put together a brief memory book with vigil stories that they then present to the family. Or they might give the family a CD of special music that they brought to the vigil.

After more than a dozen years of doing doula work and participating in hundreds of deaths, it is clear to me that the doula approach brings deeper meaning and greater comfort to the dying, their families, and caregivers. It transforms the experience from one that is fraught with anxiety, fear, and suffering into one that is filled with confidence, a sense of the sacred, and tender moments of love.

The doulas benefit as well from their involvement with the dying. Many whom I have had the privilege to train and work alongside tell me that this work is the most meaningful they have ever done in their lives. And I have trained people from all walks of life, including doctors, nurses, social workers, and chaplains. Doulas tell me that their lives have been changed by their deeper understanding of death and dying and the rewards of service. I know that their death and the deaths of their loved ones will be enriched by what they learn at the bedside of the dying.

CHAPTER 3

Death Mythology

We all carry inside us our own personal mythology about death and dying. This mythology comes from our religious and cultural backgrounds, deaths we have been close to or heard about from friends, even from depictions in literature or in the movies. Our thoughts and feelings about death aren't always completely conscious. And, because fear of death has been so inculcated in our society, we don't usually look too deeply into those thoughts and feelings when they force their way into our consciousness. But that mythology needs to be exposed and examined by the person dying and the family, or it could color their entire experience and distort their emotional reactions. One of the ways a doula can help is by facilitating such an exploration of personal mythology.

A case in point was a woman named Anna, whom I worked with when her husband, Frank, was dying of mesothelioma. She had already been taking care of Frank for two years when I became involved. Frank was just beginning to experience pain in his chest that seemed unrelated to the pain caused by his frequent bouts of coughing. I later realized that this new pain was the trigger for a myth about dying that Anna carried at a subconscious level.

Anna seemed anxious from the first time I met her. I didn't know if the anxiety was related to the stress of taking care of Frank, part of who she was, or related to earlier events in her life. Perhaps the third time I visited, Anna and I were sitting at the dining room table, which was covered with piles of papers, half-drunk mugs of coffee, and a vase of dried-up flowers that had dropped their petals like crumpled bits of colored paper. All around the house, I saw evidence that Anna had stopped taking care of anything other than Frank. That morning, she had trouble sitting still while we talked.

Every time we heard Frank coughing in the bedroom down the hall, Anna would pop out of her chair and go into the kitchen, which was separated from the dining room by a half wall with a counter. The first time this happened, she brushed at some crumbs on the counter with her hand, but didn't actually wipe them up. The next time, she turned a flame on under a tea kettle, only to turn it off a moment later. She was clearly distracted, like an injured bird aimlessly hopping around on the ground.

Finally, Frank must have fallen asleep, because we didn't hear coughing for a while. Then Anna seemed to focus more on our conversation. I began to probe into what was causing her obvious distress. She told me that Frank and she had been close friends with neighbors, Tracey and John, in another garden condominium straight across from them. John had also come down with mesothelioma, just three years before Frank. The two couples were about the same age. Although the men had not worked in the same place, they had both been in the construction industry. Anna had helped her friend Tracey as she took care of John. During the last year of his life, Anna had been there every day.

Over the last six months of his life, John had experienced terrible, unmanaged pain. By the time he died, Anna was traumatized by the agony she had witnessed every day. "He would writhe around in the bed like a fish out of water," Anna said. "Twisting himself all up in the sheets so it was hard to get him untangled. And I know we caused him even more pain straightening him out again."

When Frank started to have that pain in his chest, Anna believed it was the start of the same horrible period of pain John had experienced at the end of his life. Even though the nurse had increased Frank's pain medication and told Anna they would be able to manage his pain, she didn't believe it. Her experience of John's death had convinced her that at some point the pain medication would no longer be effective and that Frank would die in intense pain. In fact, she believed that all death ended in intractable pain.

That belief came from the two deaths she had been intimately involved with: an uncle's when she was in her thirties, and then John's. Her parents had both died in a car accident, so they hadn't had the prolonged dying experience she had witnessed in her uncle and John. Anna was terrified. "I just can't watch Frank suffer the way John did," she said. "I don't know what I'm going to do."

Her fear about what was to come over the next several months overwhelmed her thoughts, tormented her dreams, and made her irrationally angry at Frank. Her anticipation of the terrible pain Frank was going to experience drained her energy. She couldn't focus or take care of things around the house. She even found it hard to be with Frank, because she didn't want to see any more signs of what was coming.

I reinforced what the nurse had told her about the hospice's ability to manage pain, except in extreme circumstances. There was no reason to believe that Frank would be one of those rare cases. Nor is mesothelioma an illness that is associated with unmanageable pain. I even pointed out that since Frank's pain medication had been increased, he seemed more comfortable. But Anna heard the voice of her myth whispering dread in the back of her mind. It wasn't about what she saw; it was about what she projected into the future.

In that visit, I was only able to introduce the possibility that Frank's death might not conform to her past experience. It took consistently working with her myth, as Frank moved closer to dying, to finally ease her fear. Then she was able to stay with what she was actually experiencing in the present moment.

Uncovering and exploring Anna's myth helped me to understand why she was so distracted and disconnected. Part of the doula's role is to help people explore their death mythology so that it doesn't stand in the way of experiencing dying in a more engaged and meaningful way. If Anna hadn't come to accept that death isn't always terribly painful, that expectation would have overshadowed her entire experience.

Myths about death and dying tend to center on particular aspects of the process and what happens after a person dies. People's myths can impact treatment choices, the place a person wants to die, the medications they choose to accept, the way they interact with family, how they handle broken relationships, how openly they share their feelings about death, and how the body is treated after the person dies.

In the middle of a vigil for Abe, a Jewish man in his late eighties, an issue surfaced about how he was going to be buried. One of Abe's sons-in-law, Michael, wanted him to be buried according to the dictates of Orthodox Judaism. That meant that his body would be wrapped in a shroud and placed in an unadorned pine box. It also required certain prayers to be read at the graveside by an Orthodox rabbi.

Other members of the family were opposed to what Michael wanted because they believed that Abe, who had not been very religious, would not want that kind of burial. They could not ask Abe, since he was actively dying and unresponsive. The situation was made more difficult by the fact that everyone in the family loved Michael and knew he had a special place in Abe's heart.

It isn't unusual for a family to experience a clash of beliefs like this. Sometimes these clashes lead to angry, hurtful outbursts that can spark long-lasting resentment, which is why the beliefs and the stories behind them need to be examined and understood. For Abe's family, the clash wasn't angry or hurtful, but it was nonetheless very difficult, and they didn't know what to do.

One of Abe's three daughters—not the one married to Michael—asked the whole family to gather for a meeting to discuss the problem. Since I was the doula who had mainly been responsible for helping them plan his vigil, they asked me to facilitate the meeting. Late in the afternoon, while an aide sat at Abe's bedside upstairs, the whole family gathered on the deck at the back of the house that overlooked a well-landscaped yard with a small man-made waterfall that Abe had built in a mound of rocks.

I asked everyone to sit in silence for a few minutes to settle their thoughts and emotions. The sound of the waterfall seemed to deepen the stillness. Then I asked everyone to bring an image of Abe into their mind and hold him in their heart as we began our discussion.

I started by stating the main issue: whether or not to bury Abe as an Orthodox Jew. I asked everyone to follow a couple of ground rules for this family meeting: only one person could speak at a time, and when a person spoke, it would be as honest and direct as possible without disparaging someone else's idea or opinion.

I asked Michael to speak first, telling us why he believed Abe should be buried in the Orthodox way. Michael and his wife had become Orthodox over the past fifteen years. He said that he loved Abe and, according to careful study and consultation with his rabbi, this was the only way to take care of Abe after he died.

I then gave everyone a turn to state their thoughts and feelings about Michael's request. What became clear was that they all respected and loved Michael, but for various reasons felt troubled or resistant to his insistence on a burial tradition that felt foreign to them. Most of the family were not particularly religious. They also thought such a burial would be foreign to Abe, who believed in God but only went to services a couple of times a year on the Jewish High Holidays.

After the initial round of opinions, I opened up the discussion, allowing people to speak when they wanted to. At times, I would ask someone to clarify what they had said, or I would summarize a number of opinions that seemed connected. After a while, the family seemed to be moving toward a decision not to bury Abe in the Orthodox way. It was then that Michael made a very impassioned plea. "If he isn't buried in this way, his soul will be lost forever. I'm fighting for his soul." The fervor with which he spoke stopped everyone. They fell into silence. The decision they were nearing disappeared, and again they were thrown into a quandary. How could they go against such passion?

The discussion meandered for a while longer. Then I suggested that we ask Abe's wife, Mildred, to speak for him. As his lifetime companion, she certainly knew him the best and had the right to speak for him. At first, all she could say was that an Orthodox burial disturbed her. She thought it was because Abe and she weren't religious.

When the feelings about an aspect of the dying process seem strong but unclear, it helps to probe into deaths the person has experienced in the past. As I asked Mildred about her past experiences, she told the story of her first death, that of her father's father, when she was about ten years old.

"Although my parents tried to keep us away from the room where he died," Mildred related, "my older brother and I snuck over to the doorway and peered in anyway. They had covered my grandfather with a sheet and placed him on the floor, with his feet facing the doorway. Something about his covered body on the floor scared us, and we ran to my room. Years later, I saw a mummy movie in the theater, and I thought about my grandfather wrapped in a sheet on the floor. I know these associations don't make sense, but the thought of Abe wrapped in a shroud brings up the fear I experienced on those two occasions."

"What do you think it is about covering Abe up or having him wrapped in a shroud that is so upsetting?" I asked.

"I think it's about having his face covered," she said, somewhat hesitantly. "Yes, that's it. Having his face covered will take away his identity and make him feel like a thing rather than a person."

Mildred's story and her sudden recognition that having Abe's face covered was at the heart of her difficulty led to a breakthrough in the discussion. The family found a way to negotiate their different beliefs. They decided to bury Abe in a shroud, but allow his face to remain uncovered, which Michael said would be acceptable in the Orthodox tradition. They also asked Michael to say the graveside prayers when the time came, rather than asking a rabbi they didn't know.

The myths people hold may not be entirely clear to them, even though they can be extremely powerful. They may be revealed only in the way people behave or speak about death, which is why a doula's presence can be important. They are trained to be especially observant in discussions about death and the dying process.

Exploring past experiences with death should also be a part of the life review process early on. If the dying person has the energy and the cognitive ability to conduct this exploration, all of the significant experiences they had with death should be reviewed. This exploration can be conducted internally by the dying person or by working with a family member acting as a doula. But because this review can raise some strong emotions, it may be easier to do it with a doula who isn't connected by family ties or friendship.

To begin, the dying person should make a list of every death they can remember—people and animals. Identify the ones that seem most important. Then the person should tell the story of each of those deaths as it comes to their mind. The most salient parts of the experience will get revealed in the telling of the story. The doula can write down whatever seems most meaningful. The doula will also ask questions about how the experiences may have contributed to what the dying person or family member believes, anticipates, or fears about the dying process and what happens afterward. The following questions may spark this kind of examination:

- What troubled or enlightened you about this death?

- How might this death experience color your beliefs about how you will die or how you want to die?

- Were there cultural or religious beliefs you saw playing a role in this death, and how do you feel about them now?

- How did this death affect other close family or friends, and how does that impact what you want for the people close to you?

- Did that death leave you with regrets that you hope to avoid in your dying process?

- What elements of this experience might you want to incorporate into your death and why?

Sometimes it helps to create a myth that seems to tie together the experiences of death. This kind of narrative may reveal hidden assumptions that unconsciously impact behavior. When a dying client, Christine, and I explored the significant deaths in her life, the death of her mother was the most prominent. Christine had been twelve at the time.

"I remember my mother's death being peaceful," Christine said. "It was what happened afterward that changed my life. Within six months, my father remarried. I was the oldest of four, so looking back now, I certainly can see why he brought another woman into our family. But he never mentioned my mother again after the funeral. It was as if she hadn't ever existed."

Christine and I continued to talk about her relationships with her mother, father, and stepmother. We also examined what she remembered about her grief. "I felt like I didn't belong anywhere," she said. "None of my friends had lost a parent, and I couldn't talk with my dad. He never brought it up, and he gave me the clear message that I wasn't supposed to speak about it. Then, when my stepmother arrived on the scene, I didn't feel like she belonged in my family, either. She was nice enough, but she wasn't my mother."

Christine had experienced another death that was oddly reminiscent of the death of her mother. After she and her husband Craig had been married for twenty years, her mother-in-law died. Christine had felt very close to her. Within six months, her father-in-law was dating a woman he then married before the first anniversary of his wife's death. Christine saw Craig tear up at times when his mother came up in conversation with their children, but he didn't want to talk about her on his own with

Christine. When she asked him how he was doing, he would always respond with one word: "Fine."

The parallels between these two deaths were striking. Although Christine's mother-in-law never really served as a mother to her, she still represented a mother figure in her life. Both husbands married very shortly after their wives' deaths, and the deaths were not openly discussed. As we analyzed these deaths further, some of the subtler aspects also seemed to link them. For one thing, both women were unassuming and took a back seat to their husbands. For another thing, their impact on the lives of their children seemed to die with them.

I suggested that Christine contemplate how these two deaths affected her understanding of death and merge those thoughts together into a narrative myth. At points in the process she asked me to help her formulate her thoughts more clearly. In the end, the most telling part of her myth went like this:

> Death always comes at inopportune moments. It doesn't care about the devastation left behind—lives turned upside down, future hopes or plans shattered like a glass dropped from soapy hands onto a stone floor. The bitter truth is that a woman's life is forgotten quickly. Men replace them as if they were interchangeable after death. Soon the world doesn't even know they existed, and their mark on other lives evaporates like the moist impression of a kiss on your cheek.

As I listened to the myth, I could hear Christine's underlying anger and fear. She wasn't just speaking about the death of her mother and mother-in-law, but about her own death. She recognized this, too.

"When I think about Craig finding someone else after I'm gone, I get angry," she said. "I realize it's childish and selfish to wish that he never loves anyone again. I feel like I did when I was twelve. And I'm also afraid that I won't be remembered any better than an album of photographs stored in the attic."

Christine also realized that these feelings of anger and fear had been unconsciously playing out in the way she responded to Craig's efforts to care for her. She had been making him feel that what he did was never enough or done well. In a sense, she was pushing him away before he could have a chance to abandon her.

As a result of these insights, Christine was able to change the way she had been relating to Craig and open up a deep conversation between them about what would happen after she died. Exposing her hidden myth helped to change her quality of life and allowed her to work through feelings about the future beyond her death. In the end, she was able to die very peacefully.

Early in my career as a hospice social worker, I was working with a woman whose husband was dying of end-stage dementia. During one visit, I asked her about religion and spirituality. She told me that she was an atheist. So, naturally, she didn't believe there was any form of existence after death. I wasn't shocked by that belief, even though I happen to hold a different one. What made me have a visceral reaction to her thinking was the vehemence with which she expressed it. "Anyone who believes in an afterlife or, for that matter, a God is stupid and childish," she said as she looked at me intently.

Although I tried to maintain a neutral expression, I think the stiffness in my face revealed my feelings. "You don't like what I just said," she added. I stumbled my way through an attempted denial and then an apology, but the damage was done. We had to drop the subject.

Much later, I was able to bring it up again without having a reaction or bringing my beliefs into the conversation. Through this experience I learned a powerful lesson: Beliefs can turn into judgments, which will make a doula ineffective if they are revealed during the interaction with a dying person or family member.

Sometimes, people ask a doula what they would do in a certain situation or what they believe about the nature of dying: questions such as how they should deal with unfinished business, how long before the person will die, what they will experience at the very end, or what happens after death. A doula will not put forward their own beliefs but will stay right in the middle of these questions and not supply an answer. Struggle with such questions stimulates the development of answers that have great personal meaning, and may even be transformative, for the person who is asking them.

So, when pressed for an answer to some of the common questions people ask, the doula will put the question back to the person. For example, when a dying person asks what happens after death, the doula might respond with: "What do *you* believe happens?" Giving the question back to the person asking it can open an important dialog. It helps the person to continue to reflect on their thinking and even go deeper into the dilemma or anxiety that often lurks just behind the question.

If the doula were to offer their idea or belief, it might stifle further exploration. Other ways to toss a question back include: "What do you think?" or "What has your experience taught you?" or "What does your faith tradition or culture tell you about this?" Putting questions back to a person compels them to stay with their internal struggle.

The doula approach honors struggle in recognition that satisfying answers generally come only from wrestling with a question. The internal search can't be rushed. Like tasting wine, a person has to swish an answer around inside for a while to get a sense of its body, sniff its aroma for its subtler elements, and hold it on the tongue to distinguish its hidden flavors. Then they can come to appreciate its value.

If a person is stuck and can't move forward, the doula might suggest that they try on different answers and see what emotions and thoughts come up with each set of shoes they step into. At times, visualization has proven very successful in allowing a person to try out different scenarios, again asking them to feel what fits, not what they think is the most pleasing answer.

Another approach is to temporarily sidestep the question and explore what gives the person strength—the inner resources that gave them the ability to handle difficult questions in the past, their sources of resilience, and looking at whether or not they are accessing that strength or resilience. If not, why?

But the doula will also recognize when the person can't go any further—at least for the moment. At that point, it is helpful to sum up what has been discussed, review where the person is right now, and suggest some next steps to continue the process. Even though an exploration may feel incomplete, it may still be very meaningful for the person—it may open a door for them at some time in the future.

At the right moment, a doula's experience or belief might open the door to another perspective for a dying person or family member—but only after utilizing all the other approaches, and in the hope that the person will explore the doula's perspective and digest it internally.

Earlier I wrote about my father's death and the guilt I felt after missing his last breaths. That experience has certainly contributed to my mythology about death—informing my thinking about the importance of being present for the last breaths. There are times when I share that experience as a way of offering an idea that might further a discussion between a dying person and the family about being present at the end.

Sometimes, however, people give up in the face of questions that seem too difficult or perplexing for them. Then the doula will find a way to be supportive and nonjudgmental. Ultimately, compassionate, loving support is even more important than finding the answers to troubling questions.

Family and caregivers also need to understand this. For them, it may be more difficult to accept that their loved one simply can't go further in finding or accepting an answer to a question they have struggled with. In families, we tend to push one another into beliefs, especially if we think the person would be happier thinking something different. But this can make the dying person feel worse and resent the person doing the pushing. So family members have to find in their hearts the ability to support their loved one, no matter where they are in confronting the inevitable questions they have as they approach death.

CHAPTER 4

Truth Telling at End of Life

Too often in facing the end of life, the truth about diagnosis, prognosis, and treatment is held back from the person dying. This begins a pattern of withholding information, obfuscation, and secrecy that only increases the isolation and emotional suffering of a person at the end of life. Medical professionals bear a great deal of the blame for the avoidance of truth, because they have the responsibility of informing patients about their prognosis— a responsibility they hedge with talk of hope, percentages for response, and the latest treatment options. But the phobia about death is woven tightly into the fabric of Western society. So a person with a terminal illness and the family can hardly be faulted for turning away from the truth and holding on to miracles.

When family withholds the truth from the person dying, their rationale may be to keep the person from falling into a state of depression, even despair. They want their loved one to hold on to hope and savor the aspects of life that can still bring pleasure or joy. I have heard many family members say something like this: "The truth will only keep them fixated on death. I would rather they enjoy the time they have left. And, if that is at the price of bending the truth or even misinformation, so be it."

But this reasoning is based on several false assumptions. First of all, truth, even bitter, difficult truth, doesn't necessarily condemn a person to unrelenting sorrow. Truth can be freeing. Yes, it may initially cause sadness, but accepting death can inspire deep inner work and healing of relationships.

Jack received a diagnosis of abdominal cancer in his early fifties. He endured years of various chemotherapy treatments. At first they seemed to hold his cancer at bay, but then his illness started to progress again. Finally, his doctor had to admit, "There's nothing more I can do now."

Jack's wife, Sheila, was surprised at how well Jack took this news. His mood was much more upbeat, in contrast to how sad she felt in the days that followed. Over the next several weeks, Jack talked about trying to build himself back up and regain his lost energy. Yet most days when Sheila came home from work she found him snoozing on the couch. He would say that he hadn't felt very well, but tomorrow he would push himself. Only the next day and the next, it was the same story.

Sheila began to wonder if Jack had really understood what the doctor had told them or if he was in extreme denial. She asked one of her closest friends what to do. That friend told her to let Jack hold on to whatever illusions he had about getting better, so he wouldn't get depressed. Although she felt that her silence was like lying to Jack, she followed her friend's advice.

She could tell, however, that her daughters, who were in middle school and high school at the time, were confused by what was going on. Sheila was afraid to talk to them. She thought the truth would make them sad and change how they related to their father, which could puncture Jack's denial. She also didn't want her daughters or Jack to feel that she had given up on him.

More weeks went by. Sheila felt that she couldn't live with the deception any longer. She called the doctor to ask if he would talk to Jack again. "I think Jack didn't understand from our last visit that he's going to die," Sheila said. "When you told him there was nothing more you could do, you added the word 'now,' and I think he heard in that a future possibility of treatment and getting better."

"I believe Jack knew what I meant; most patients know the truth even before I say it," the doctor responded. "I don't like to take hope away from my patients, and I don't think you should either. Hope is a good coping strategy. Besides, we never know when a new chemotherapy will come along."

Sheila asked how long he thought Jack had if nothing changed. He told her three to four months—maybe six—if the cancer kept growing at the rate they saw from the last CT scan. Sheila felt a stabbing pain in her chest. She hadn't expected such a short prognosis. She realized that even she hadn't fully accepted her husband's condition. But now that she thought back over the last several weeks, she recognized how much Jack had declined.

During the next couple of days, the devastating truth of what she, Jack, and her girls faced darkened every one of Sheila's waking moments. She saw that the secret she carried, and Jack's denial, made it impossible for them to have a serious conversation about anything. An avalanche of denial had buried them all, and she didn't know where to dig first to get them out. At last she decided to talk to Jack. They cried together, talked openly for the first time in many weeks, then told the girls. The next day, Sheila called the local hospice.

Shortly after going on hospice, the nurse talked to them about the doula program they offered. That's when I started visiting. Even though they had broken through the wall of secrecy about Jack's impending death, there were a number of occasions when they fell back into the habit of denial or shaded the truth from other people, even from themselves. I could see when this was happening and would probe their thoughts and feelings until the truth rose to the surface.

With denial a thing of the past, Jack and I began a series of visits centered on life review and exploring meaning. As we pursued this, Jack came back over and over again to the sadness of realizing that he wouldn't be able to watch his young daughters grow up and move into their own lives.

"I feel like I'm abandoning them before I've had a chance to help them discover who they are," he said to me on one occasion. He also felt that dying was a betrayal of his marriage to Sheila. They had promised each other a time when they could travel and enjoy each other after the girls were on their own. Now that would never happen. He worried about how her life would be when he was gone.

As we worked through these feelings, Jack decided to write letters to his daughters to express his love, to tell them how proud he was of who they were becoming, and to express his wishes for their future. He also wrote to Sheila to tell her how much he loved her, to thank her for always supporting him, being his best friend, and taking such good care of their children. He told me that he also asked her not to remain alone but to find someone she could love. "Just maybe not as much as she had loved me," he said with a smile.

He included in the envelope a pendant he had bought for her upcoming birthday but would not be able to give her himself. He had asked his sister to have it engraved with a special message. He asked me to deliver the letters a few weeks after his death, when I did the reprocessing visits with Sheila, the girls, and other family members.

Jack went through an amazing transformation in the last weeks of his life. His relationships were never more loving. Sheila and the girls spent an incredible amount of time with him. Even with his continued decline and the changes in his face and body, he always seemed joyous. Everyone felt it when they were at his bedside. He told me he was grateful to the cancer for teaching him how to appreciate every moment and helping his family to learn that as well. He was truly at peace. One of his daughters told me she felt like they were living inside a rainbow.

From denial and secrecy, Jack and Sheila had traveled a long way into a place of great openness and acceptance. They had broken through the taboos surrounding death and allowed their young children to accompany them for the whole journey. In doing so, they had modeled for their daughters a way of approaching death that can bring joy and peace in the midst of anticipated loss.

Almost every person I have worked with during the dying process ultimately comes to appreciate that truth works out so much better than clinging to secrecy and denial. Truth liberates people to do healing work, take charge of the last days of their life, and create lasting legacies. Avoidance of truth creates only a façade of normalcy that stunts interactions and leaves family feeling empty and regretful.

One of the most frequently stated justifications for lying to the dying is that it will take away hope and replace it with dread and depression. But that isn't what I have seen in my career as a hospice social worker and doula. In fact, I believe people have the picture upside down. When families lie to their dying loved ones—and to themselves—they create more suffering and worse outcomes.

As happened for Jack, some period of initial sadness often gives way to relief that everyone can speak openly. And the greater benefit is the possibility for a death that truly honors the person dying and surrounds them with love that can only be offered when people aren't holding back in fear of the truth.

Secrecy and misinformation rob a person of their right to live their last days as they choose. It robs them of their opportunity to experience a sense of completeness, to deal with unfinished business, to offer and receive forgiveness, to express love. And it robs everyone else of the ability to share their most heartfelt feelings with the dying person while that person can still receive them.

Truth telling isn't only about knowing one's diagnosis and prognosis. It is also about the truth of facing difficult pieces of a relationship or dealing with unfinished business. When a person is dying, we really need to clear the decks of all the debris from past storms. To die well, a person should have the opportunity to deal with all those issues, even the ones that linger from years before.

It is hard to die peacefully if a person hasn't dealt in some way with the regrets, guilt, discord, and brokenness from the past. No matter how long ago a troubling event occurred or how many difficult words were spoken, there is always a way to lessen their impact—perhaps even to bring healing. That might happen directly or through a letter—one that might never even get delivered. The expression of regret, clarifying a situation, or offering forgiveness can be extremely powerful and transformative for all involved. Just a few words intended to heal a rift or a difficult relationship can be enough.

When I worked with Edith, she was in her early nineties. She didn't have a major underlying illness, but it was clear that her body was failing. Her children were cold and unloving toward her because—as she told me quite openly—she had been a terrible mother. Throughout their childhood, Edith had failed to give them the attention they craved. All her energy had gone into throwing parties for friends and entertaining her husband's business associates. Only after her children were fully grown, and had children of their own, did Edith realize how badly she had failed them. Although her children visited her occasionally, they never spent much time or shared their lives with her. She hardly ever saw her grandchildren.

As we did the work of summing up her life, it was clear that this huge failure hung over her death with the weight of a mountain. It preoccupied her thinking and brought her unrelenting anguish. Life review sessions always led back to this guilt and pain. Edith had timidly tried to bring up this issue with her children, but they would quickly shut her down and refuse to hear her out. She had no peace.

So, after much discussion, Edith decided—without me suggesting it—to write a letter to each of her children to express her overwhelming sorrow at failing them as a mother. She agonized over each letter for many days. Finally, feeling very unsure of herself, Edith asked me to read the letters and tell her what I thought.

I remember sitting in the living room of her very fancy midtown apartment, surrounded by 18th-century paintings, marble floors and columns, Persian rugs, and polished antique furniture—the accumulated evidence of wealth generated over a lifetime. But none of it mattered to Edith as much as the withheld love of her children. The letters were incredibly painful but beautiful and heartfelt nonetheless.

Edith didn't try to explain or justify herself. She didn't hold back. In each letter, she spoke about the strengths she saw in the child to whom she was writing. In each letter, she asked them to give her a chance to show how much she loved them. She didn't ask for anything in return. I told her the letters were perfect.

I was away on vacation with my family on the Saturday Edith invited them all to come for dinner. The home health aide who lived with her was going to make a traditional French Guianese meal. She had told me that she intended to hand the letters to her children as they left.

I thought about Edith and her letters often on my vacation. I had become quite fond of her and wanted things to go well. When I visited her a week after she had given the letters to her children, I was immediately struck by the lightness I saw in her. Each of Edith's children had called her after reading their letter to tell her in one way or another that they were touched by what she had written and would try to open their hearts to her. One of her daughters had already visited again, telling Edith in tears that she had hoped for this for years, but she had been too scared of getting rejected once again to bring it up herself.

Although Edith's children had scars that wouldn't just disappear, they and she were able to feel that the walls between them had crumbled a little. The last months of her life were filled with love she had never expected from her children and grandchildren. Breaking through to the truth had been a gift for all of them.

Truth has power at the end of life. It can lead to healing, transformation, and peace. Doulas encourage truth, because it can have a profound impact on the dying person and the rest of the family. Doulas also speak the truth whenever they are asked for it. For it is only through trust that people can open up and tell the truths they may need to speak before they die.

CHAPTER 5

Deep Active Listening

Probably the most important thing anyone can do for a dying person and their loved ones is to truly listen to them. The activity of listening is at the heart of the doula approach. It allows a person to share their fears, regrets, frustrations, longing for God, brokenness, love—the whole swarm of emotions and thoughts that buzz around inside them. For someone to share these deeper parts of themselves, they must feel that they will not be judged, have their feelings changed, or have ideas imposed on them. This act of true listening—what I refer to as "deep active listening"—lays the foundation for all emotional and spiritual support. It is a gift of compassion that family can give to a dying person and to each other.

To listen in this way, doulas put themselves aside and stay open to what the person has to say—without fear, without a personal agenda, and without letting their own feelings get in the way. A doula doesn't turn away from something that is difficult to hear, challenges their beliefs, or forces them to examine their own ideas or feelings.

Even at a surface level, listening well isn't as simple as it may seem. Most of us have acquired some poor listening habits. We listen with only part of our mind, while the rest of it thinks about a host of things unrelated to the present moment. We focus on how we are being received. We jump in to share our own thoughts or experiences before the other person is finished speaking. We imagine that we understand without checking that we have it right or clarifying what we heard. If we manage to pay attention to the person, we only listen to the words and miss what they say with their body, the expressions on their face, the intonation in their voice.

To avoid stumbling into these poor habits, we must listen "actively." True listening is not a passive activity. It takes focus. The listener has to remain open and return to listening when they get pulled away by an unrelated thought or a distracting stimulus. A good listener has to look for openings to explore beneath the surface of what a person says, periodically check their understanding, read the nonverbal cues, stay aware of their inner reactions, know when to allow silence, and stay alert for insights that may come from their intuitive mind.

Centering

Good listening begins well before the first words are uttered. It starts by shifting out of the busy mind we carry around with us at all times—a mind filled with thoughts and feelings like schools of fish that change direction in an instant and swim rapidly in every direction. Imagine that you are at a lecture, trying to hear the ideas being presented, but a couple next to you doesn't stop talking the whole time. That couple is your busy mind distracting you and interfering with your ability to hear the lecture. A name for the act of shifting out of busy mind is "centering."

There are many different approaches to centering. As a student of Zen Buddhism, I find that meditating on breathing is an approach that works well. Perhaps ten or fifteen minutes before I visit a dying person or the family, I will meditate on my breath as I sit in my car or walk down the street to where the person lives. If I'm sitting, I will focus my mind on the physical sensations of my breath in my lower belly or at my nostrils. If I'm doing walking meditation, I coordinate each breath with the stepping motion of one foot after the other, concentrating on the sensations of raising and lowering my legs and the contact of my feet with the ground.

At times, I will add a short phrase spoken internally and softly as I breathe in and out, a practice that comes from the teaching of Thich Nhat Hanh. For example, breathing in, I might say: "Present moment." Breathing out, I would say: "Only moment."

Another approach utilizes guided imagery, also called visualization. I will explore guided imagery more thoroughly in chapter 9. For now, I want to describe a centering visualization.

For this visualization, a person sits with their eyes closed, so they can move more easily into the imagination. They start with a minute or two of breath meditation, then call up the image of a still pool of water—perhaps in a forest. Then they visualize sitting at the edge of the water watching its surface. A frog jumps in, creating ripples that move outward in all directions from the plop of where it entered the water.

As the person continues to watch the surface of the water, the ripples slowly dissipate until the pool is completely still again. The person gradually becomes that stillness. When they feel ready, they open their eyes and carry that stillness and the receptivity of the pool in their mind as they enter the person's home or room.

The busy mind can be very insistent. Thoughts, memories, sounds, or bodily sensations will drag a person away from their focus. Each time that happens, just return to the centering practice. The activity of returning over and over again to the breath, or to a mental snapshot of the still pool, will keep them centered as they prepare to listen to a dying person or family member.

Centering stills the mind and accesses intuition that may help a person see things not obvious to the upper layers of consciousness. But a person also needs to open outward to listen deeply. One approach to opening outward is to turn the focus to every sound a person can hear in the space around them. In this part of the preparation, it's essential for a person to maintain some portion of their focus on the breath at the same time that they listen intently to every sound. It is this dual focus, awareness of what is happening inside as well as outside, that is most effective for listening deeply.

The last part of centering is to set an intention to let go of all expectations and goals. If a person is caught up in wanting to make something wonderful happen, is anxious about saying the wrong thing, or has an agenda related to a particular issue, then they are too caught up in concerns about themselves or their ideas about what is needed to truly listen.

Family members will have to distinguish between times they intend to listen to their dying loved one and times when they may need to bring up an issue or raise a concern. It is often hard for family to separate these two activities. A doula can help with this. For a dying person to speak openly and freely—particularly about deeply meaningful or emotional subjects—they must know that their family member is there at this time to just listen. This can be so critical as the dying person faces their final days.

After setting an intention internally, I find it helps to verbalize that intention out loud. There is something about speaking it, even though I'm alone in my preparation, that seems to give it weight and power; that makes it feel like a commitment I intend to strive toward.

As I do this part of my preparation, I will hold my hands with palms together in front of my face or heart, which comes out of my Zen practice and symbolizes for me that the giver and receiver, or the listener and speaker, are not two and not one at the same time. This gesture with the hands is also a sign of gratitude for whatever will be offered.

The Visit

When a doula enters a person's home or room, they begin the engagement with a dying person or the family. How they do that will set the tone for the rest of their visit. If they are an outside doula, they may begin by telling people who they are, the purpose of their visit, and how long they anticipate the visit will last. If a family member is spending some special listening time with the dying person, or with another family member, they need to make it clear that this time together isn't about socializing or discussing everyday matters, but rather an opportunity for the person to speak about deeper issues, explore meaning, or plan for the vigil. The first few minutes of a visit help establish a level of comfort, build trust, and demonstrate the person's willingness to stay open to whatever needs to be said.

In the end stages of an illness, physical decline can occur rather quickly, emotions can shift suddenly like a wind shear, or family dynamics can cause draining explosions of anger. So, before addressing deeper subject matter, a doula will make sure that the dying person isn't struggling with a physical symptom. They will also check to see if the dying person is too tired or too preoccupied in some other way to be engaged in the visit. If the visit is primarily with a family member, then the doula will ensure that the person isn't too stressed or tired from recent care demands or too overwhelmed by family dynamics or upcoming events to talk.

If a doula thinks that a visit should be cut short, for any of the above reasons, they will suggest coming back at another time—unless of course the doula is there to take a shift during the vigil. There is no point in pushing someone when they can't be truly present. Before leaving, the doula might just sit with the dying person for a while, offer some light hand massage, or do a visualization to help them relax.

Deep active listening doesn't mean sitting back and saying nothing. Even in the early part of a conversation, a dying person or family member may need to talk about something that is delicate or very emotional for them. The doula will recognize this need and stay calm and centered. If the person speaking lapses into silence, the doula won't rush to fill that pause. Silence is often very fertile. The person might need to reach down inside for greater courage to go on, or to find the right words, or simply to check on their level of trust. Silence is an appropriate moment to follow the sensations of breathing for a breath or two, repeat a centering or listening phrase, or visualize hands with the palms together.

Before a doula responds to what was just said or takes the conversation in a new direction, they may ask: "Is there anything more you want to say about that?" That opening might encourage the person speaking to go further or deeper into what they said. The doula might reach out and touch the person at this point, if they know it's okay. Touch can help show warmth and compassion.

Going Further

Even when listening deeply, it's possible to mishear what a person says or not understand what they meant. This happens more than you might suspect. Sometimes it happens from lack of patience. Sometimes the filter of an agenda distorts what is heard. Sometimes expectations, assumptions, or projections get in the way. Also, particular words or modes of expression may trigger reactions for the listener that come from their cultural background or personal experience. Whatever may be the cause, the result is the same: the person speaking isn't really heard, and if they sense that, it may affect their willingness to speak in the future.

"Reflecting back" is a helpful technique. It involves the listener, in their own words, telling the person speaking what they just heard. The listener can use some of the same language, but the reflection shouldn't just parrot what the speaker said.

Reflecting back creates a verbal pit stop in a conversation. The listener checks on understanding, the speaker clarifies if necessary, then the listener checks their understanding again. A great deal of misinterpretation is avoided using this technique. Also, when a speaker has to clarify what they said, it gives them a chance to crystallize their own thinking and see even more subtle layers of the subject. It's like traveling on a spiral staircase, swinging around to nearly the same perspective but also moving further along. The dance of give and take between the listener and the speaker brings them closer together and creates a profound empathy.

In the process of reflecting and clarifying, the listener may experience moments of intense emotion that can't be held back. Sharing emotion demonstrates that the person is walking the path of dying along with everyone involved. It is okay to show emotion, as long as the response does not shift attention away from the dying person.

Naturally, this technique of reflecting back isn't appropriate at every twist and turn in a conversation. It should be saved for those important moments, when checking understanding is critical and deepening the conversation through clarification may lead the dying person to discover something significant. Even through the process of reflecting back, the doula will praise insight and courage where they can. That might provide the extra energy a person needs to keep struggling through doubt, indecision, and confusion. These actions are what make active listening "active."

One of the hardest things for family to do when they attempt to just listen to their dying loved one—and to each other—is to refrain from trying to soften the edges of suffering, bring light into the dark, solve a problem, or remind someone of the goodness and joy they experienced in their life. Even trained doulas find it difficult to resist the impulse to fix a situation or solve a problem. But allowing a person to struggle gives them the opportunity to find their own answers, their own wisdom. Then the resolutions they arrive at are truly meaningful and satisfying.

Allowing struggle is an act of true listening. But the person struggling must feel that the listener is able to stay with them through the process, supporting them in their journey toward an answer. There is a story I was once told that I think exemplifies what it means to stay with someone in their struggle.

The parents of a teenage girl, who was out of control at home, brought her to a therapeutic wilderness program. Because she was fighting against going to the program, the parents had taken away her shoes and everything she would normally carry with her—including money and a bank card. The only things the girl had were the clothes she was wearing. The program would outfit her when she arrived.

At the meeting place, the girl refused to get on the bus that would take her to the main campsite. She simply walked off down the street of a town she didn't know. One of the counselors told her parents they would handle it and they should leave. As they pulled away, they saw a counselor walk down the street after their daughter. Only later did they find out what had happened.

The counselor caught up with the girl and began walking alongside her, not saying anything at all. I was surprised as I heard the story that the counselor didn't start talking up the program and try to convince her it was going to be great. He didn't talk about how much success they'd had, how it would turn her life around. Nor did he tell her that she really had no other choice under the circumstances or try to frighten her about being in a strange place with no money. He just silently walked alongside her.

After another couple of blocks, he did something that I thought was inspired: he took off his shoes and continued to walk alongside her in his socks. She couldn't help but notice, but she didn't say anything. The two of them just continued to walk along. After maybe another half mile, she finally turned to him and said, "So, you aren't going to leave me alone, are you?"

"No, I'm going to stay with you," he said.

A few minutes later she said, "Okay, let's turn around." On the way back, she started to really open up about what was going on in her life.

If the counselor had tried to talk her out of her anger or assure her that she would like the program—in other words, deny the feelings she was having—she would not have trusted that he really cared about her. He would be just one more adult who didn't get it and was only concerned about compliance, not her feelings or struggles.

In a similar way, a doula won't try to change the feelings of a dying person or family member. If they did, the message might be that they can't handle intense emotions nor see issues and problems from someone else's perspective. This story about the teenage girl and the counselor demonstrates how a doula walks alongside the people they serve. In a metaphorical way, doulas take off their shoes—that is, remove the boundaries we erect to protect our hearts—and stay open to anything the person needs to talk about, without trying to change their feelings or fix the problem.

The doula will accept and normalize feelings, then explore their underpinnings. Only when the person demonstrates in some way that they are ready to do something about the feelings or related issues will the doula offer assistance, suggest a solution, or try to shift their perspective.

To walk alongside someone through active listening, the doula stays patient and trusts in the other person's capacity to handle their feelings and find their own wisdom. If at some point the person struggling can't find their way forward, the doula will offer a suggestion, framed as a choice that honors the person's autonomy. When a decision is made, a path chosen, or the person just decides to give up, the doula leaves judgment aside and supports the person where they are.

Over time, deep active listening becomes an established part of the relationship between a doula, a dying person, and the family. When a doula arrives for a visit, or a family member sets up some special time to listen to their loved one, people just naturally move into the patterns of true listening. The trust developed by listening without judgment deepens the engagement between a doula, the dying person, and the family.

In that atmosphere, people naturally feel more comfortable talking about the difficult aspects of facing death. Now a dying person might talk more openly about their fear of dying, anger at God, anxiety about the future of family members, frustrations over the losses they have already experienced, unfinished business, and the disappointments, failures, regrets, or guilt in their life—the fundamental anguish and existential dread at the root of many a dying person's suffering.

For the same reasons, and in similar ways, family will find it easier to talk about their emotional exhaustion; the pain of watching their loved one's body, mind, and spirit wasting away; and the suffering they will experience as they witness the end stage of the dying process. Family will also find it easier to discuss their anger at God, the illness, perhaps even at the person dying for not taking care of themselves well enough to avoid their illness.

Putting It Together

Before arriving at Anthony's house for my first visit with him, I parked around the corner to spend a few minutes centering myself. I didn't want to park in front of his house and have the family wonder why I wasn't getting out of my car right away. I meditated on my breath for a few minutes before shifting part of my focus to the sounds around me. Then I set my intention. Feeling focused and open, I drove the last bit to Anthony's house.

In my mind, before getting out of the car, I did one last thing that comes from my Buddhist training: I offered up to Anthony, his family, my other patients, and all dying people the good that might come out of this visit. In Buddhist terms, this is called "giving away merit." This brief practice is also my way of reminding myself that the visit is all about this dying man and his family—letting go of my ego's needs to do well and be liked.

I already knew some things about Anthony from talking to his social worker and nurse. He had worked for the Department of Public Works in his town. Almost everyone who knew him appreciated his dedication to maintaining the local roads, his devotion to his wife and four daughters, as well as his generosity to neighbors. Often after work he would go over to someone's house down the block to fix a leaky faucet or repair a broken lawnmower.

Anthony, who was dying of lung cancer from a lifetime of smoking cigarettes and cigars, lay in a hospital bed in what would be considered the "front parlor." The bed was in front of a big picture window that looked out onto the street, so he could see all the activity for a stretch of the block and in front of the houses across the way. This strategic placement of the bed reflected the importance of the neighborhood for Anthony. It felt like he was as much out there as he was inside his house. He later told me that all three of the houses I could see across the street had had the same occupants for the last forty years. His block was equivalent to the small village in Italy that his family had come from.

Whenever I enter someone's home, I look around at the objects displayed, the furnishings, because these things speak of the people who live there and help me begin to understand them. For Anthony, his window out onto the street spoke as much about him as the pictures of his grandchildren that were sitting on the credenza and hanging on the walls.

His hand when I shook it felt thick and hard like a piece of wood. I couldn't imagine how he felt anything through that skin, which had been toughened by a lifetime of hard physical work. His smile was broad and almost childlike. His wife and four daughters were clustered on a couch and chair across from his hospital bed—his rooting section and protectors.

After introductions, I checked on how Anthony was feeling that day. His first response was "fine." One of his daughters pushed him a bit. "Come on, Dad, tell him how you're really feeling."

I watched his face as she spoke and checked inside myself to see if I was picking up his feelings. I had this sense of discomfort. I suspected that he didn't like talking about how he felt or being seen as complaining. I didn't say anything in the silence that ensued, waiting to see if he would speak or if his family would speak for him. I wanted to see more of the dynamics between them. When he didn't speak, the same daughter that had prodded him told me that he had no energy and barely got out of his bed now. We talked a little more about his physical state and how the family was doing, where everyone lived, and about the grandchildren.

There were no immediate issues that needed addressing, so I launched into an explanation of the doula program to make sure they understood it. Everyone was clear that they wanted the doulas. After that, the family left Anthony and me alone so we could talk more personally. I began as I often do with as big an open-ended question as I can. "So, tell me about yourself."

"Well, you've already met my daughters," he started. "There isn't much to say beyond that. Mary and I were the third couple to buy a house on this block after they were built. And the first two couples still live right over there," he pointed directly across the street.

What people choose to talk about first is often as revealing as the information they provide. Clearly family and neighborhood were how Anthony defined who he was to an outsider, and likely to himself as well. It also confirmed his self-effacing nature.

As the conversation went on, I had to continue to ask questions, taking on a more active role than I might have with someone else, because his answers tended to be brief, even though my questions were open-ended. But I kept trying to turn over the direction of the conversation to him. After a while, I could feel his growing comfort with me. So I tried to open the door to a deeper level of concern.

"I want to understand what is important to you now, given where you are in your illness, and how you want to spend the time you have left," I said. "When you sit here alone and you aren't distracted by your family or what is going on outside, what do you think about?"

"I think about my garden," he said.

"Tell me more about that."

"At the side the house, running all the way back to the property behind us is my garden. I've been growing vegetables there since the first spring after we bought the house. My neighbors will tell you that I grow the best tomatoes they've ever eaten. I give more of them away than we keep—but there's still plenty to last all summer and for my wife to make into sauce we can use throughout the rest of the year." This was one of the longest answers he had given me.

"I'd love to see the garden at some point," I said.

"Cathy [one of his daughters] can take you out there before you go."

"What is it about the garden that makes it so important to you now?" I asked, continuing to use open-ended questions to move further into his concerns.

"I don't have the energy to get out there anymore, and I'm worried about how the garden will do without my attention."

"Are you afraid the garden won't produce as many or the same quality of vegetables without your personal touch?" I asked, reflecting back what I believed he was saying.

"Yes, that, and I know the family and my neighbors look forward to the vegetables. I don't want the garden to die because I'm dying," he said, both clarifying and taking the meaning further.

"I can feel how sad that makes you," I said. This was the first time I had named or talked about an emotion. I wanted him to see that I was in touch with what he felt, even if he didn't speak of it directly. I wanted him to know that I was willing to walk alongside him wherever our conversation led. "What do you think you can do about that?"

"I'm not sure. What do you think?"

"Well, that isn't for me to say." I wanted to let him know that he needed to figure this out—if he could. My role wasn't to solve his dilemma but to return him to his struggle. "What have you already considered?"

We explored this issue more, but he didn't come up with a solution that day. Two or three visits later, he told me he had arrived at a solution. He decided to teach his daughter Cathy and her husband how to tend the garden exactly as he would. He and the family found inventive ways to get him out there a few times, so he could help them to learn how to feel and smell what the soil needed. He made them promise to keep making the abundance of tomatoes a source of cohesion for the neighborhood. Over time, this dilemma about his garden became the key to exploring his values, discovering what he had learned in his life, and creating a legacy project that would preserve the garden and its meaning to him for future generations.

One of the last times he was able to be in the garden, Cathy's husband made a video of him directing her and other family members how to create raised beds for later plantings. Then they also asked him to speak about moving to the house and what his early life was like on the small New Jersey farm his parents had owned.

As I hope Anthony's story makes clear, active listening doesn't mean that all a doula does is listen. At the right moment, they may make an observation, suggest a range of solutions, or share an experience. This will be done only after careful thought and when the moment is rife with possibility. Even then, the doula will try to encourage an organic process of self-discovery.

A doula will share deeply in peoples' emotions, so the dying person can feel them walking alongside them in their pain. But the doula will maintain a thin boundary so the dying can own their death. Like the finest of lace nettings around a bed in the tropics, the boundary is nearly transparent but maintains the separation the fabric provides. The boundary also protects a doula from absorbing the suffering they must bear witness to in the dying process.

Doulas use the skill of deep active listening throughout their work with a dying person and the family—in the series of pre-vigil visits, when they help explore meaning, discuss legacies, and plan for the last days; during the vigil; and in the reprocessing sessions after death. All emotional and spiritual support depends on the kind of connection active listening nurtures between a doula and the people they serve. Even the tools of guided imagery and ritual are grounded in active listening.

CHAPTER 6

Life Review and the Search for Meaning

Questions about the meaning of one's life arise quite naturally as a person approaches death. The questions center on how well a person feels they have lived, the things they have accomplished, how happy they were, and the impact they had on others. These questions often arrive in the middle of the night when the dying person can't sleep or in those moments when activities around them don't hold their attention. Usually, these questions do not result in a careful examination of events, because people do not appreciate the benefit of doing that. Instead, they surface and disappear in fleeting moments, like silvery fish jumping above the surface of a stream and falling back in.

Only when a person explores these questions in a serious and concerted way will they resolve the basic conflict that Erik Erikson delineated between ego integrity and despair (discussed in chapter 2). A dying person can either ignore that developmental challenge or face it head on. The doula approach advocates for engagement, because we have seen that successfully resolving this challenge helps a dying person achieve wisdom and peace at the end of life.

Life review is the primary tool a doula uses to guide the dying person in exploring questions of meaning. One of the main theoreticians on life review was Dr. Robert Butler, who wrote about the need to process experiences from the past so that a person can reintegrate them in a positive way. Research prompted by Butler's work demonstrated that life review can reduce depression, increase life satisfaction, and promote greater acceptance of self—results that support healthy ego integrity.

In my work with dying people, I have found that the most powerful and insistent memories tend to revolve around unresolved conflicts, guilt, regret, and blame. It is easier to explore those kinds of memories after establishing a relationship of trust with a dying person. Sometimes, however, even in an initial visit, the painful memories are right there and need to be worked on immediately. This happened during my first visit with Richard, a man in his late sixties who was dying from pancreatic cancer.

Richard's wife led me across a marble floor to an unexpectedly small living room crammed with furniture, vases, sculptures, and paintings that covered nearly every square inch of the walls from floor to ceiling. The effect was claustrophobic and dizzying, as if the room could suddenly start spinning on its own axis. Richard was huddled into one corner of a couch covered in a wild print fabric. As we went through the introductions, he handed me a framed picture of himself standing confidently on a ski slope somewhere. He was solid looking and large framed but not heavy.

"That was me before I got sick," he said. "I hardly recognize myself now when I look in the mirror." The man sitting on the couch looked half the size of the man in the photograph.

"You look like you belonged on the slopes," I said.

"I was an excellent skier. Every winter I would go to Europe at some point to ski in the Alps. It was one of the ways I indulged myself," he said, his voice heavy with nostalgia. "Now, I can hardly move off this couch to get to the bathroom. One of the few pleasures I have left is watching the leaves on the Japanese maple out there [he pointed to the one window in the room] as they dance in the wind. They look like they belong on a bird rather than a tree."

I was sitting on a chair in front of the couch. I didn't say anything, waiting to see if he would speak again. I could feel a pensive sadness in the slow way he spoke. It was clear that there was something on his mind that was larger than the decline in his body. As I discussed in the chapter on active listening, a doula will allow silence, especially in moments that seem charged— like this one did.

"I've been thinking about so many things in the last several days," Richard said. "Failures from the past and regrets haunting me. How can I come to terms with that at this point? It feels overwhelming."

So here we were, entering the zone of life review work at Richard's initiative. When this happens as organically as it did with Richard, the doula will allow the person to control the direction of the conversation, because it comes from an urgency inside them.

"It sounds like you're thinking about the negative things that happened in your life; things you wish you could change. Is that right?"

"Yea, it's all the places I messed up. Maybe I'm thinking that way because I'm staring into the face of death. You can see it in my body; it's getting closer."

"Would you like to talk about some of that now?" I asked, still not sure if he was ready to do life review work. I wanted him to decide.

He seemed to grow smaller as he sat there, gazing once again out the window. I knew better than to interrupt the inner calculation that would lead to whatever he needed to say next. As I waited, I saw signs of physical pain play across Richard's face. He rubbed the right side of his abdomen below the ribs. I chose not to ask him about the pain just then, because I didn't want to divert him from his internal process. But I wondered if worsening pain was contributing to the urgency he felt to talk about the negatives in his life—a sense that time was running out.

When Richard did talk again, he started to tell me the story of his first marriage. He had been in his mid-twenties. He said that his wife periodically experienced deep depression, which dragged him down into dark moods he had never experienced before. At some point, they had started fighting a lot. He realized after a few years of this that he didn't love her anymore, but he couldn't bring himself to end the relationship. The crucial decision points in life, those times when a person chooses one direction or another, and the reasons they make those choices, reveal a great deal. They can become the focal points in exploring meaning and, later, in expressing that meaning in a legacy project.

Choices lead to outcomes that may be positive, negative, or a combination of the two. When a person does life review work, they need to explore choices, events, and outcomes. Discussion about negative outcomes or events will reveal some of the work a person might do to resolve conflicts that stand in the way of turning toward integrity and away from despair. Talking about the positive outcomes or events will reinforce integrity and may lead to possible legacy projects. Looking at both leads to uncovering meaning.

As it turned out, it was the choices in his first marriage and their outcomes that caused Richard the greatest pain in his life. His second marriage, which had produced two daughters who were very close to him, had brought him only joy.

When a person does life review work, it helps if they cover all the periods of their life to discover the seminal experiences that drive their overall sense of success or failure. Typically, I find that the middle years of adulthood tend to contain more of those, so I usually start my life review there, asking questions that are pointed toward the main activities of life: work, relationships, socializing, involvement with spirituality, and time spent alone. The questions should be open-ended, such as: "Tell me about your work." "How did spirituality or religion play a part in your life?" "What felt satisfying or disappointing about the work you did?" One of the broader questions I like to ask, because it often uncovers unfinished business or unresolved conflicts, is: "What difficulties did you encounter in your middle years?"

Without me needing to ask the question, Richard had led us directly into a conversation on probably the biggest difficulty in his life. A difficulty that, when he looked back on it now, involved a series of bad choices and painful outcomes. It took us a couple of visits to fully explore those choices and outcomes. They involved having a child against his better judgment and staying in the marriage too long.

"When I finally left," Richard told me during our second visit, "my wife turned bitter and nasty. I was the sole support for them. I tried to stay involved in our daughter Jennifer's life, but my wife made that more and more difficult. By the time she was in her mid-teens, I saw Jennifer only sporadically, and she made it clear she didn't care if I visited."

"That must have been very painful," I said.

"It broke my heart. But by then I was remarried and had young children who loved having me around. At one point, due to circumstances and the demands of my successful business, I didn't see Jennifer for six months. When I thought about calling her, it just felt too hard, so I didn't. I only heard from Jennifer once, about five years later. It was a very angry phone call. She accused me of abandoning her and blamed me for everything that was wrong in her life. Now I haven't seen or spoken to her in over fifteen years. This is the big failure in my life. It haunts me now as my death gets closer."

At this point Richard looked straight at me, and I could see the suffering in his eyes. When someone is in such despair, it doesn't help to try to immediately change the feelings, to find some way to soften them or push them aside, like hosing dead leaves off the walkway to your house. I knew there was much in his life to be proud of. But often when a person approaches death, it is the failures or the regrets that speak most insistently in the mind.

"I think about Jennifer all the time, like a tune you can't stop hearing," he said. "And the thoughts seem to get louder and more insistent. I try to think about the good things in my life, but the guilt and self-blame won't let go of me."

"It sounds like trying to replace your troubling thoughts with more positive ones isn't working. Have you thought about other ways to deal with this?"

"I have thought about trying to get in touch with her. But even if I could find her, I'm terrified that she wouldn't want anything to do with me. That would be so devastating at this point. How could I carry that into my death?"

Up to this point in our work together, my role as the doula was to help Richard explore the issue that was plaguing him and allow solutions to come from inside his struggle. Now I felt the time was right for me to make a direct suggestion that might help him move in a direction he had considered but was afraid to try.

"Of course you don't know what could happen. But you are certainly suffering a great deal now. Taking some other action might at least let you stop beating up on yourself so much." I placed my hand on his arm, so he could feel my support at a physical level. "Maybe trying to get in touch directly isn't what you need to do. Other people I have worked with who had to deal with a broken relationship found that writing a letter to the person was very helpful. Something about the familiar format of a letter makes it feel like you actually communicated, even if the letter never gets sent or the person never sees it. I know people who wrote to a parent or sibling who were no longer alive, and still it felt like they had communicated. It may let you unburden yourself more."

This was the beginning of a process that moved Richard out of the despair he was stuck in to working toward a resolution— or at least toward easing his pain.

After writing the letter and rewriting it a couple of times, he decided to actually try to get it to Jennifer. One of his other daughters, Lisa, searched the Internet and found Jennifer's address. So Richard sent the letter.

As we waited to see if she would respond, Richard agreed to try a visualization to release some of his guilt. I had him imagine that his guilt and shame were dark clouds that had gathered inside his chest, surrounding his heart. He could see the edges of his heart turning grey. Then, in his imagination, I came to him and handed him a jar with magic salve inside. I instructed him to rub it on his chest above his heart and watch as it turned into an opalescent light that penetrated his skin and turned the dark clouds to ones that were white and healing. He could see his heart turning a vibrant, glowing red and feel it filled with love for those around him, for Jennifer, and for himself.

I guided Richard in this visualization many times over the next three weeks. We also continued to do the life review work. Now that he had taken action on his unfinished business regarding Jennifer, he was more available to explore other aspects of his life. If there are powerful negative issues overwhelming a person, it is difficult to have them explore the more positive parts of their life experience. Once the negative issues are addressed in some way (and just listening deeply may be enough), it becomes easier to turn from despair toward integrity. Then, discussing successes, accomplishments, and joyous events will accelerate the movement toward integrity.

When Richard finally received a letter from Jennifer, she said she would come to see him the following week. The visit was very awkward and uncomfortable for everyone. The conversation skirted the real issues between Richard and Jennifer. Through the tightness in the way Jennifer spoke, they could feel the anger inside her. As a result, the visit felt stilted and unsatisfying. Lisa walked Jennifer to the door and asked her to please come back. She told Jennifer that many times in the last few months, Richard had expressed his great sorrow over what had happened; that he desperately wanted to somehow make it different before he died.

Jennifer did come back a couple of weeks later and finally expressed her anger and hurt. Richard took it all in and told her how sorry he was to have caused her such pain. The visit didn't resolve the feelings, but Jennifer kept visiting. During the last four months of his life, Richard was able to bring a degree of healing to his once broken relationship with Jennifer. I don't know how the relationship might have developed if they'd had more time with each other, but at least there was a relationship.

The life review work with Richard moved into new territory. He had come to an accommodation with the broken part of his past, which allowed us to talk about the things he was proud of, his most satisfying experiences, and his love of snow and the mountains. The shift in his emotional state was dramatic. Even though he kept moving toward his death, he was more alive inside.

He made a video legacy in which he spoke about the values he had tried to live, the things he had come to believe were most important in life, what he had learned—even through his mistakes and failures. He told everyone, Jennifer included, how much he loved them and what he hoped for them after he was gone.

The video was only about thirty minutes long, but it summed up his life in a powerful way. When I watched the video, Richard looked larger to me than the shrunken man I had met at my first visit—more like the image of him on the ski slope in the picture he had showed me. In the end, in spite of the great pain he had to deal with, he died very peacefully.

Each person, as they face their death, has regrets, brokenness, failures, and missed opportunities to examine. They may choose to simply look them over and let them go, or they may decide, as Richard did, to try to heal them. Only some people have intense issues that will preoccupy their life review and overwhelm their attempts to find meaning. The work of the doula is to guide a dying person to a place of engagement with their life experience. To open the door to understanding. Out of the crucible of that engagement will come an overall assessment that places the person on the side of integrity or despair.

If despair predominates, a doula can assist the person to find ways of dispelling its negative energy so that greater light can enter the search for meaning. However, it may not happen. If the forces of despair are particularly strong, then the person may not be able to work past them. As someone hoping to bring comfort, the doula may find it very difficult to accept this fact. So remember that the person dying owns their journey to the last breath. And even though despair may be the ground over which the journey proceeds, a doula will keep supporting that person in every way they can, then let go of the outcome.

When Sean was dying, he confessed to me that he had been a "real bastard" in his life. He was a New York City policeman who cheated on his wife over and over again. He also implied that he had done other unspeakable things that he couldn't even talk about. His own assessment of his life kept him from wanting to think about meaning. Somehow finding meaning to him sounded like covering over the wrong and the pain he had caused. He couldn't allow himself to do that. He believed that he needed to suffer, right up to his death. That was the punishment he felt he deserved.

He did at one point discuss some of his infidelity in a meeting with his wife and myself. Of course, she was well aware of his affairs. She could not forgive him—nor do I think he would have allowed that—but she was able to still care about him and for him. Even that he struggled against accepting.

Although Sean was not interested in summing up his life, or even planning for the last days, he still wanted the doulas. He hoped that his wife and children would create a plan that would help them through his final dying process. The doula approach is about providing guidance and support in whatever ways are helpful and appropriate for this particular dying person and all the people most directly involved. I felt very sad for Sean. But, ultimately, I had to accept that this was his path into death.

Many times, I have heard other end-of-life care professionals say that a person dies the way they lived. While I accept that there is some truth in that idea, I have seen people find redemption and transformation in their dying, which completely upends the story of their life up till then. So I've learned never to give up on the possibility that a person will suddenly, unexpectedly discover grace, like rummaging through an old trunk in the attic and finding an unknown family heirloom.

Sean's vigil was very brief. He started actively dying one evening and died mid-morning the following day. As a Catholic, he believed in God's judgment after death. It was as if he wanted to hurry to it, because then perhaps he would have the punishment he felt he should get.

The search for meaning often leads back to a person's childhood. That is where the person may find the roots of their happiness or unhappiness. During the life review work a doula did with Lorraine, a woman dying of colorectal cancer, she asked

Lorraine to consider this question: "What were your parents' weaknesses and strengths?"

One of the weaknesses Lorraine identified was her parents' rigid refusal to do anything that might involve taking a risk. In every decision they made, safety and stability were the primary concerns. Her parents had both come from childhoods of poverty, so this approach to life was understandable. But it also meant dismissing Lorraine's fascination with and talent for drawing, instead encouraging her to pursue a career in teaching or nursing.

However, Lorraine rebelled against what she considered the "stodgy" example of her parents' lives. That resulted in a great many arguments and long periods of unhappiness in her childhood. In spite of that, she continued to draw at every opportunity. She was captivated by the patterns that she saw in the veins on leaves or the bark of trees. She drew the insides of flowers, the groupings of rocks in a stream, the patterns of lichen on rock walls—the less conspicuous patterns of nature. She would get lost in class during high school, drawing patterns she saw when she closed her eyes tight, forcing red and yellow shapes to fill her internal landscape.

Lorraine didn't become a famous artist, but she did have a very successful career in fabric design. She took many risks along the way, including starting her own design firm. In the end, she had the satisfaction of knowing that the patterns her company created became the window coverings and wallpaper in some of the finer homes and corporate offices in the country.

As her life review progressed, and the focus shifted to her adulthood, the doula asked Lorraine about her major relationships. Since Lorraine had been married three times, the doula asked, "What did you learn from those marriages?"

"Now, as I look back," Lorraine said, "I realize that I picked men who weren't very stable. I guess I was attracted to risk in more ways than in just my career. I learned that there is a price to pay for taking risks. Nonetheless, I wouldn't change any of it. I loved freely, had some great adventures, and experienced more of the human heart than most people."

With the doula's assistance, Lorraine came to understand a truth about her life that she hadn't fully recognized before: it wasn't risk that drove the decisions she made but passion. And, when she followed her passion, even if that caused her difficulty along the way, it ultimately led to intense happiness. Passion was like a sparkling vein of amethyst running through the rock of her life.

For Lorraine, the search for meaning led to deep understanding. It helped her to see very clearly the wisdom she had acquired over her lifetime. She didn't have children, but she did have nieces who she hoped would take the example of her life and not be afraid to follow their passions. Particularly because, as young women, they would be up against what is still a male-dominated society. That was the legacy she left them.

"When I went to the viewing for Lorraine with the doula who had helped with the legacy work, Lorraine's niece came over to say hello and thank us for the services the doulas provided. Doulas often attend the viewing or funeral for people they work with. It gives them an opportunity to say goodbye internally to the person at the same time that it continues the involvement with family. Sometimes, the sharing at these events is a prelude to the reprocessing work that will come later. It also gives the family their first chance to offer their gratitude.

After thanking us, Lorraine's niece told us that she and Lorraine had a long conversation about a month before Lorraine died. In that conversation, Lorraine had talked about the realizations she'd had as a result of the life review work.

"I always knew that Aunt Lorraine was different in a really good way," the niece said. "But I don't think I framed it around the idea of following one's passion. I wanted you to know that following my passion will now become my rallying cry. It is the least I can do for Aunt Lorraine. It will be my way to keep her alive inside me."

CHAPTER 7

Creating Legacy Projects

Legacy is the impact a person has had—conscious or unconscious—on the people and world around them. Simply by living, a person has impact. In being a part of a family, raising children, participating in a circle of friends, going to work, taking a role in the community, in every sphere of life, a person leaves their imprint, just as walking across wet cement will leave footprints that solidify and remain.

Most of the time, a person moves through the events of their life without thinking much about their legacy, in the same way that they probably didn't consider meaning. But in the doula approach to end of life, meaning and legacy are two of the most important elements preceding the time a person will start actively dying. They are what lead to a sense of integrity or despair. In doing work around legacy, just as in the search for meaning, life review is the primary tool. In fact, it is hard to pull apart work on meaning and legacy. The two are inextricably interconnected. Life review serves both at the same time.

So, in the early life review work, the questions a person ponders will lead toward meaning but also toward legacy. Further along in the process of exploring, the goals of the two separate. Legacy is generally more concrete and easier to see, while meaning takes insight and synthesis. Like in an archeological dig, legacies are the shards of a clay pot, the image of a deer painted on the remnant of a wall, a broken piece of a beaded necklace. They are what people leave behind. Meaning is how all these objects fit together to reflect the way a people lived. The archeologist digs in the earth for both at the same time, using the same tools. But they are different ways of looking at the same artifacts.

The search for meaning is primarily for the person who is dying and generally occurs in solitary moments of inner reflection or on the pages of a journal the dying person writes. Meaning work also occurs in special conversations with one person chosen as a partner in this exploration—whether that is a family member or a professional doula.

Legacy, on the other hand, is primarily for the family and is often done by a number of family members in combination with the dying person. As the doula assists a person toward understanding meaning, ideas for legacies naturally surface.

Legacies may take the form of a book, a box, a scroll or a series of letters, a quilt or a fabric wall hanging, a construction in wood, a mosaic made from broken crockery, an audio recording, or a video. I know of legacies made from a path in the woods or a labyrinth that gets walked over and over again—perhaps preserved in a series of photographs on a wall in the family home. The form a legacy takes is limited only by the imagination and creativity of the people who fashion it.

A scroll made from paper or fabric is one of the more beautiful legacy projects created through the doula approach. The idea for legacy scrolls came from a bat mitzvah I attended years ago, well before I thought about the doula approach to end of life. The girl celebrating her transition into the adult world of Judaism had made a poster depicting the things that she felt were important to her at that time in her life.

Up on the dais, two of her friends unfurled a long, rolled-up piece of oak tag that revealed cut-out images of a guitar, shoes, a pop idol of the day, as well as pictures of a waterfall, a hungry child, and other things I can't remember now. The girl had also pasted on the scroll brightly colored feathers and a cloth patch from her soccer league. When it was fully unfurled, the girl pointed to each image or object to explain why it was included and how it related to who she was as a person, as well as how she hoped to impact the world as she moved into her adulthood.

I had never seen anything like it. After the service, the girl told me that her rabbi had suggested the scroll project. So I asked the rabbi where the idea had come from. He told me it was based on a German Jewish practice from four hundred years ago. After a child was born—particularly a male child—the mother would make a cloth belt out of her baby's swaddling cloth to go around a Torah. These belts, called "wimples" (which means "banners" in German), served to hold the Torah scroll together.

Sometimes the belt was made from a piece of fabric cut from a dress belonging to the mother. The wimple was decorated with the baby's name and genealogical information, and often included sewn or painted scenes that came from stories in the Bible or everyday events in the community. Some wimples included the image of a wedding canopy, in hopes that the child would marry someday, continuing the family line and helping the community to survive. So the wimple expressed the identity, past, and wished-for future of the new life.

The wimple was made soon after birth and used to wrap the Torah when the baby was first brought to the temple. It could also be used during other ritual occasions, collected by the rabbi as an artifact of the community, or passed down in the family.

I was fascinated by that bat mitzvah scroll and the history of the wimple. So, years later, when I began focusing on helping people create legacy projects, it occurred to me that a poster in the form of a scroll on paper or fabric could make a wonderful legacy. A scroll might express important aspects of a person's life in pictures, collages, or in words. It could speak to the things a person valued, accomplishments in their life, how they wished to be remembered, and their vision for the future of their family. I also love the fact that the original wimples were made from swaddling cloth, because that reminds me that the origins of the end-of-life doula approach lie in the work of birth doulas.

One of the more intriguing aspects of a scroll is that you can unfurl and display only a portion of it for a time, then roll that part up and display another portion. In Japan or China, the owner of scrolls depicting a landscape or everyday scene will hang one for a while, then put it away for a time to hang a different one. By continuing to change what is hung, they reengage with the images with fresh eyes. Life scrolls the dying person creates can be used in the same way as different sections are exposed, helping family reengage anew with that portion of their loved one's life.

When Andrea was dying from ovarian cancer, she decided to make a scroll. There was something about a long sheet of paper that symbolized for her the "river" of her life. She wanted to depict the things she cared about, like playing music (she was a violinist), hiking in the woods, her love of animals, and the need to protect our streams, lakes, and oceans. She also wanted to depict the role of serendipity in her life. She told the doula who was helping her many stories of this mysterious force that seemed to happen at crucial moments in her life.

Andrea related that serendipity had played a major part in her marriage to Peter. They had met in their early forties and were married for barely eighteen years when she was diagnosed. It was the first marriage for each of them. When they met, Andrea had just started a new job teaching music at a private high school. She had literally run into Peter—who taught English there—while going down the hall to the cafeteria. A week later, Peter asked her out for a hike, using the excuse of helping her to learn about some of the local countryside and the community.

As they shared stories about their lives, they discovered that they had been in the same place at exactly the same time multiple times in their lives without meeting, until the day they ran into each other in the hallway of the school. It was as if life kept throwing them together until they could finally meet. They married just four months later.

Andrea spoke about how serendipity continued to play a role in her life with Peter after they were married. There was the time that Peter was offered a new job at another school in the town where Andrea's sister lived. Shortly after they agreed that he should accept the position, they learned that Andrea's sister was suffering from an extremely debilitating case of Lyme Disease and could really use Andrea's help. Or the time that Andrea was invited to join a violin quartet, only to discover that the husband of one of the other players was a close childhood friend of Peter's with whom he had lost touch. Through Andrea, and the force of serendipity in her life, Peter was able to reestablish a wonderful old friendship.

As Andrea's concept for the scroll took shape, the doula suggested that perhaps a series of lines running down the whole scroll in waves and intersecting at intervals could symbolize those moments when different events or people in her life came together, seemingly but not really by accident. At each of those junctures, Andrea, Peter, the doula, and friends would place an image that represented what that moment or event meant to Andrea. Sometimes, one of Andrea's artistic friends would draw an image. But they also used collages, sewed or pasted small flat objects onto the paper, or used hand-painted or handwritten words to clarify the meaning.

Working on the scroll gave Andrea purpose, even as she continued to decline. Legacy work often functions in this way. As people move closer to dying, they can feel as if they are just waiting to die. They aren't able to do much for themselves and feel they don't any longer have a role to play in their families. They don't see a purpose.

But when people work on a legacy project, they regain a sense of purpose. They now have something very productive to do, or direct, that not only brings them and their families together, but also provides a platform for funny or touching interactions with real substance. It also lets the dying person see that there is a future for them that goes beyond their body. The legacy project will serve as their voice in the future and allow family to continue to engage with them and their legacy.

As the work on Andrea's scroll progressed, she realized that she wasn't afraid to die, because she believed that the universe would not have brought her and Peter together to tear them apart without some future possibility of being together again. For her, the force of serendipity was a message that death wasn't the end.

"I know I will be with Peter again," she said to the doula. "I believe we were together in earlier lives and will be with each other in many future lives."

When the scroll neared completion, Andrea and Peter made imprints of their hands in paint on the scroll, their forefingers and thumbs touching. Andrea asked Peter to hang the scroll on the wall across from her bed so she could keep seeing it. Every few days, Peter would open up a different section of the scroll and close others. At the ends, they had attached wooden dowels to make it easier to roll up or unfurl it. The doula had suggested that they keep space at the end of the scroll so that they could add to it later—even after Andrea died. When Andrea took her last breath, Peter wrote the time down in the middle of her handprint on the scroll. Although he hadn't thought about it before, Peter also asked everyone present at Andrea's death—even the doula—to sign their names to the scroll.

When the doula visited Peter to do the reprocessing, he pulled out the scroll and stretched it across the living room floor until it was totally open. He and the doula walked around it to point at their favorite images and discuss their importance to Andrea.

The doula returned several times over the next three months to continue the reprocessing. Between the visits, Peter, his sister-in-law, and some of his close friends continued to work on the scroll. It helped him process his feelings and work through the early part of his grief.

Finally, he agreed with the doula facilitating the reprocessing meetings that it was time to finish the reprocessing work and the scroll. Again the scroll was rolled out in the living room, which was now filled with candlelight. Peter played Andrea's favorite violin music, then asked each person there to write two or three words from their heart to Andrea. Peter added the final words on the scroll, using a paintbrush and Andrea's favorite color, green: "Until we meet again."

The content of a legacy project can center on a single important aspect of a person's life or a host of things that mattered to them or to the people around them. That content may come from identifying the things that were most important to the person, major events in their life, values they held, things they learned in life, their relationship with family and friends, accomplishments, involvement in the community, their work to change society, and on and on.

Above all, the legacy project should focus on how the dying person hopes people will remember them or the messages they wish to speak into the future—perhaps to continue influencing the people who go on after they die—in other words, the emotional, intellectual, and even spiritual inheritance that family and friends receive because this person was part of their life. This form of legacy is much more valuable than the money and objects a person might pass along.

In contemplating the content for a legacy project and trying to see the best way to narrow its focus, a dying person may also reveal things about meaning in their life. The two play off each other and impact each other in a back-and-forth dance of discovery. In the act of shifting from thinking about content to the form that will capture that content, the process shifts from an inward focus to one that is oriented outward. People in the family may contribute at this point in the process, bringing their own perspectives and enriching the project.

When Susan thought about her legacy, food immediately came to mind. Over the course of her life, she felt most alive in the kitchen. It was the place her day began and ended. She loved the sights and smells of cooking, the time alone with her thoughts as sauces simmered away on the stove, or the give and take with her husband and children as she put them to work cutting, chopping, or mixing. There was an easy comradery among them when they prepared, cooked, and cleaned up together. No one fought during cooking.

The kitchen was the hub of their family life. The kids had done their homework there when they were young, the family ate all their meals there, they played board games there after dinner on the weekends, they entertained friends there, and there they celebrated important holidays. The center of gravity for the family was the mahogany dining table that stood solidly in front of a wall of windows in the kitchen.

Food was also one of the first things people thought about when they thought of Susan. She never made a bad meal. Her food was uniformly delicious and healthful. She often brought food to friends or baked for neighbors. She even felt disappointed when plans with friends involved eating out in a restaurant.

People asked Susan for recipes all the time, but she had a hard time giving them, because she never measured anything. She felt or saw the right amounts of ingredients. It was as if she could taste in her mind exactly what this pinch of a spice would mean to the overall flavor of a dish, much like a great composer can tell exactly what notes from the oboe will contribute to the overall sound of a symphony. Susan learned this free-form style of cooking from her mother and grandmother, both of whom cooked in exactly the same way.

The only question was how to express this importance of food for Susan in a legacy project. One of Susan's sons suggested a recipe book, because there were dishes he wanted to learn how to cook. Everyone liked the idea, but then, of course, there was the problem of how to record the ingredient amounts. They thought that they might solve this problem by cooking a select number of dishes together and photographing every step—including close-ups of amounts Susan held between her fingers or cupped in her hands, the height of the flame under the pots and pans, the order in which things were added.

That led to the next problem: How could Susan work at the stove when she couldn't stand for more than a few minutes, due to weakness from her disease progression? After some research, they found a walker with a seat that was higher than a tall stool. It allowed her to stand with arm supports when she could and sit when she needed to, while still being high enough to see into the pots and stir the food.

They decided to limit the number of dishes to a half dozen of their favorites. Still, it would take several weeks to accomplish even those few dishes. As they thought more about the project, they decided to expand the concept to include pictures of them eating the meals together, which of course is the point of cooking the meals in the first place.

The project kept growing as they worked on it. One of Susan's sons decided to research some of the spices they used. For example, paprika is the main ingredient in Chicken Paprikash, a family favorite they included in the book. Although this dish is associated with Hungarian cuisine, variations of it come from the Ukraine and Russia, where Susan's maternal relatives had lived generations earlier.

They discovered that paprika actually originated in Mexico and was first brought to Spain by Christopher Columbus, then later introduced into the Balkan region by the Ottoman Turks. Susan's son wrote some of this history into the margins of the pages devoted to the Chicken Paprikash recipe, along with the few early sepia photographs of Susan's grandmother, who had taught Susan how to make it.

So what started as a simple recipe book became a much richer project, with family history and a history of ingredients woven together with family photographs and images of sharing food. It isn't unusual for projects to grow in this organic way as they unfold. It is one of the beautiful aspects of working on a legacy project.

Susan's project served to preserve an important part of who she was throughout her life. It brought the family together at a time that their impending loss might have strained relationships. It helped them to appreciate Susan as part of a historical chain of women that kept family tradition alive. Susan also began to understand how food was a reflection of deeper values she held: the primacy of taking care of family, generosity in offering nourishment to friends, placing the needs of others above her own needs. The legacy work actually led her back into exploring meaning at a level she hadn't experienced up till then.

Everyone who worked on the recipe book came to realize that it would become one of those family treasures passed down for generations. It would help Susan's immediate family reconnect with her after she was no longer with them physically. It would inform future generations about their roots, allowing them to appreciate where they had come from.

The legacies that people create are as varied as the people who make them. They don't need to be huge, complicated, or artistic. They need only to express some aspect of who the person has been, their role in the family or community, and the impact they may have on the future life of the family.

The process of creating a legacy project has important benefits to the immediate life of the dying person. It gives them a sense of purpose and fills time that could feel empty with positive thoughts and actions; it allows them to stay connected to who they are at a time when their sense of self might be shattered. I have noticed that working on a legacy project can even lessen pain, nausea, vomiting, anxiety, and depression.

The satisfaction from seeing a completed artifact that the person knows will speak of them and for them in the years to come is tremendously gratifying. It is the ripple of their life continuing to shape and form the future. It is a gift to those they love.

Legacy work also has immediate benefits for family. As they get involved, it allows them to engage more with their loved one in a substantial and positive way, which can totally change the nature of their interactions. As a result, they feel less anxiety, fear, depression, and anticipatory grief. It also helps family to cope better with the suffering they may see at times and gives them a natural opportunity to offer and accept words of forgiveness and thanks.

All of these positive outcomes for the family tend to continue into the bereavement experience after the person dies, lessening the pain of loss and allowing a deeper healing.

When the doulas started working with Phyllis, she was already weak and seemed to have little interest in the world around her or her family. She was sleeping a great deal. To her husband, Cliff, it felt as if she had given up and was just waiting for the end. It felt the same way to Phyllis and Cliff's daughter, Marilyn. "I know my mom is dying," she said. "But she has withdrawn so much that it feels like she is already gone. And I think it's depression, not the illness."

At first, the doulas also struggled to engage Phyllis in conversation. She would keep her eyes open for a little while but drift away and then close her eyes. Marilyn was the one who helped the doula learn about Phyllis. "My mom loved to throw parties and entertain," Marilyn told the doula. "It was the way she showed her love for everyone, and that's exactly how people experienced her parties—an evening of Phyllis lavishing love on them."

Phyllis had made every family event special and attended to every detail. Nothing was too minor to have her loving touch. Marilyn recalled how every one of her birthday parties had a different theme. When Marilyn had graduated high school, her mother had a party for her friends and the whole family. At every place setting, there was a story about something Marilyn had done that was funny or reflected the person she was growing into.

Before the meal was served, everyone took a turn reading the story that was at their setting. People laughed uncontrollably over the funny stories—some that Marilyn didn't even remember. Other stories made people well up with tears.

This story of Marilyn's graduation party gave the doula the idea to suggest the family collect stories about Phyllis and put them into a book. The doula and Marilyn talked with Cliff, then they asked Phyllis what she thought about the idea. At first Phyllis said no, because she didn't like to be the center of attention. But when the doula helped her understand that the project was really for everyone else, she relented. Marilyn took charge of the project and ran with it. It felt so good having something productive to do, to have a way to honor her mother.

The project began with a list of all the people the family wanted to reach out to for their stories. The list grew quickly. Marilyn couldn't contact everyone on her own. Since she didn't have children, she turned to her nieces and nephews, who were thrilled to help. They all worked together, using email, the phone, and Skype. Stories came handwritten through the mail, others through email, and some were dictated to a person acting as a scribe. Without being asked, people started sending photographs as well—some that Marilyn and Cliff had never seen before.

In her excitement over the project, Marilyn started sharing some of the funnier or more touching submissions with Phyllis. On those occasions, Phyllis stayed more focused and engaged than she had been during the previous couple of months. It was clear now that Phyllis's lack of energy and sleepiness were part of her disease process, but the project had brought her back to them. She would share her recollection of a particular story, add details, and laugh over the funnier ones. She couldn't do too much at a time, but she contributed memories of her own and told Marilyn where to find photographs that might get included in the book.

One day, Marilyn showed Phyllis a wonderful picture: Phyllis and four of her friends on a shopping expedition. They were each wearing an outrageous hat and had hammed-up expressions on their faces. Phyllis laughed and laughed.

"We did have so much fun that day," she said. "You know, life wasn't always easy. Your father and I had times when we had to dig deep to make things work between us in the early years; money was tight, and you kids were certainly challenging at times. But through it all, we never lost our sense of humor or ability to have fun. If there is any one piece of advice that I would give people—my legacy, as you call it—it would be: 'make sure you have fun.' You will find happiness to the extent that you keep having fun."

Later, those words, "Make Sure You Have Fun," would become the title of Phyllis's memory book.

When the book was done, Marilyn asked the family to get together so they could all see the final product. Marilyn and her sisters-in-law made a meal for everyone to share. Phyllis could barely eat at this point, so they puréed her food. Marilyn placed Phyllis at the head of a table that held thirty-five people. Before Marilyn served the meal, she asked one of her nieces to bring out the book and hold it up so that everyone could see it.

Beneath the title, the cover had a collage of Cliff's favorite pictures of Phyllis, which he had personally selected and merged together using Photoshop. As the niece held up the book, she said, "Grandma, in this book we put the stories we collected about you. They tell how much love and joy you brought into everyone's life. This is our way of thanking you and holding on to you forever." Then the girl handed the book to Phyllis so that she could see the photo collage better and feel the weight of all her stories.

Cliff was sitting next to Phyllis to help her through the meal. He took the book from her and read the story he had written about their first date, when he had picked her up on a borrowed motorcycle. Phyllis's mother and father had been aghast and threatened not to let her go, until Cliff's politeness won them over. After that first story, dinner was served.

When the dinner was done and the table cleared, Marilyn took the book and read the story that followed the one her father had read. Then the book was passed along from one person to the next, each reading a story. Marilyn later said the room seemed to expand with each story, yet she felt a deep, reverential quiet fill the space beyond the words read. It reminded her of a feeling she'd had once when she climbed down into a subterranean Anasazi Indian ceremonial room called a "kiva" at Mesa Verde National Park.

Some of the stories were funny, most were touching; they all expressed the incredible love that everyone felt for Phyllis. "Whenever anyone was with my mom, they could feel the joy inside her and they felt good," Marilyn said. "She just exuded this warmth of spirit that people felt immediately. If you spoke to her about something that wasn't going well in your life, she made you feel that it would be okay—you didn't have to worry about it anymore."

The stories seemed to swirl around them, joining with one another to create a panoramic view of Phyllis's life and personality. They all felt the connection to Phyllis and one another in a palpable way. Cliff remarked on how special the evening felt. He looked over at Phyllis's face frequently and saw how moved she was.

What a gift they had given her, to let her hear directly from each person the sweet memories they carried of their times together. It is so rare to give stories back to a dying person. Cliff thought they would all hold on to the memory of the evening, and how it fed Phyllis, in a way that would make their grief lighter.

After the last person read from the book, everyone spontaneously stood up and applauded Phyllis. It was a beautiful moment of honoring the life she had lived and the place she would hold in all their hearts for the rest of their lives. It was a moment of the highest integrity in a life nearing its end. Exhausted, Phyllis went straight up to her room and bed. Cliff sat at her bedside for a while, holding her hand and gently stroking her face. He said that her face glowed and smiled even after she had fallen asleep. Downstairs, everyone continued to talk about how amazing the stories were and how beautifully the book had turned out.

Just three weeks later, Phyllis started actively dying. Throughout the two and a half days of her vigil, the book sat on a night table by her bedside. From time to time, one of the family, a friend, or the doula would open it up and read one or more of the stories. Occasionally, another story would come to mind as a person sat alongside Phyllis, and they would write it on one of the blank pages that had been left at the end.

After Phyllis took her last breath, those present gathered around the bed. The doula took out a letter that Phyllis had written in secret for this moment. The doula read Phyllis's words out loud. The letter talked about how full her life had been due to all the love from family and friends. She expressed the truth that she lived by: taking care of our relationships is the most important activity in life. She also thanked them for the night of her stories when everyone had read to her. She said those few hours were among the most precious hours of her life, and that in the days afterward, it hadn't felt to her that dying was so bad.

At the memorial service held for Phyllis a week after her death, in the front of the funeral home room, the book of her stories sat alongside the urn with her ashes. Marilyn said at the reprocessing visit weeks later that seeing the ashes and the book together had spoken to her of a mystery about life that she hadn't seen before that moment.

"The body that housed my mom was just a container that could be reduced to ash," she said. "Her real life existed in the loving energy she generated and shared with all the people she encountered. That energy could not be destroyed or diminished by the death of her body. In fact, it could continue to expand outward through all the hearts that carried her memory or would still come to know her through the stories in the book. Her legacy was love."

It is ideal to have months or at least weeks to do legacy work. The more time spent on a legacy, the greater the benefit to the dying person and the family. But circumstances don't always allow for that. If a person is already actively dying before any legacy work has started, then simple is better than elaborate—at least during the time of the vigil. Family will want to focus on being present for their loved one and will probably find more involved legacy work too distracting. Presence at the bedside and rest when they need it should take precedence over legacy work.

However, simple legacy work can still provide opportunities for family to engage with the fullness of a dying person's life, even as the focus has narrowed to watching for changes in the breathing. One of the easiest legacy projects, which works well when started during a vigil, is collecting stories at the bedside. Many families have simply placed a basket or a box on a night table, along with writing or drawing implements and paper or blank index cards.

When a person spends time at the bedside, they can take a few minutes to write down a story or something the dying person said to them. Or they can express their feelings about the person, their wishes for the vigil time and the time afterward; anything that comes from the heart. They can use color or draw images to enhance the messages they leave.

These small, unstructured deposits of memories and wishes begin to take on the weight of legacy. Later, when the family is grieving, they may take these writings and incorporate them into a book or a scroll. But even if they choose to leave them as a collection in a box, the stories can have profound value to the family.

Legacy work doesn't even need to start before a person dies. Family may find that creating a legacy project becomes a way to engage with their loved one's life as they grieve. This can help them fully explore and come to appreciate the emotional and spiritual inheritance the person left to them in the form of changes to who they are and the residue of memories.

Anne Carson, a Canadian poet who teaches ancient Greek language, created a legacy book about her brother after she learned that he had died. Her brother had had a troubled life, and there were periods of years when Anne and her mother didn't even know where he was or if he was still alive. A replica of her legacy book, which she did as part of working through her grief, was published in the form of an accordion book—long sheets of paper pasted together, then folded into pages in a continuous stream from the first page to the last. In a way, this format mirrors the nature of our lives: an unbroken flow of moments, separate yet connected.

The book, called *Nox* and published by New Directions, is a compendium of writings, torn bits of letters on airmail stationery, simple drawings, collages, photographs, and in some places, single words that feel as if they were stabbed onto a page, surrounded by dark scribbles of pain. It is a powerful elegy to Anne's brother and evidence of the impact of his life and the mysteries he left behind.

So even with sudden death, legacy work can have a great impact. It becomes a tool for understanding that person's life, a way to reveal its meaning, a way to honor them. And no matter what form the legacy project takes, it becomes a concrete artifact of that life, allowing people to reengage with the person who died, and a reminder of how people continue to carry them inside their ongoing lives.

Like essential oils that are distilled from a plant or the rind of a fruit, a legacy project captures the concentrated fragrance of a person's life, its sweetest flavor, its most vital characteristics. It is the way a dying person goes on beyond the life of their body.

It is the way their life continues to play across the surface and depths of other peoples' lives. Finally, it is the way we begin to comprehend that there is no such thing as death, no matter what may or may not happen after the last breath and a stilled heart.

How sad it is that so many people die without ever having the opportunity to examine their life and explore its meaning in this way; to move consciously toward integrity and arrive at a sense of completion. How sad it is that as a person approaches their death, they don't have the opportunity to hear directly from their friends and relatives what they meant to them. How sad it is that most dying people don't know that their legacy will be preserved and maintained. Through meaning and legacy work, a person comes to understand themselves, and they get to model for others how we come to terms with death.

CHAPTER 8

Planning for the Final Days

Planning for the last days of life is another important aspect of the doula approach to caring for the dying. Most people don't plan, because they try to stay focused on the immediate care demands and sustaining as much of their normal daily life as possible. These tactics help everyone keep thoughts of death at bay. It is like walking along a narrow ledge of a mountain pass; you don't look over the edge to contemplate how high you are or what would happen if you fell. Instead, you watch the ground a little bit in front of you and pretend this is just a normal stroll in the outdoors. Otherwise, you could lose your balance or become immobilized by fear.

Another reason people don't plan for the end of an illness is that they don't understand the choices they have or the benefits of planning. Instead, they feel that all they can do is suffer through the experience, hoping it ends as quickly as possible.

Medical personnel involved in care of the dying don't usually inform them and their family about the choices they may have.

That isn't their professional orientation. Rather, they tell people what to do, teach the family about medications and the basics of physical care. The rest they leave to the vicissitudes of the illness. In contrast to that, doulas encourage thinking through all the choices about where a person dies, what the room will look like, the feeling of the space around the bed, and the kinds of interactions people want with each other and professional staff.

When a dying person and the family plan for the last days, they feel less afraid and less anxious. They regain some of the sense of control that the illness had robbed from them. In addition, a doula will raise questions that people don't generally think about. So not only do they feel better prepared for those last days, but they also see how the plan they create deepens the sense of meaning in the dying experience.

The Environment

Most people prefer to die at home, if possible. They can be surrounded by the things they love; there are no institutional rules they have to follow; and they feel more comfortable and safe. The desire to die at home is usually a primary factor in choosing to go on hospice care. Today, perhaps 75 percent of patients on hospice service do die at home. Out of the remaining 25 percent, some die in the hospital because they panic and call 911. For the rest, it is a matter of choice to die in a hospice facility or hospital for symptom management issues, cultural preferences, caregiver breakdown, or the presence in the home of an emotionally fragile child.

When the dying person and the family have determined the setting, the next consideration is how the room will look.

Naturally a person can control the environment more when they are at home. But even in a hospital room, there are ways to make the environment feel less institutional and more personal. Since many deaths occur in the hospital or nursing home, this is an important consideration. And just because a person is dying at home, that doesn't automatically guarantee that the space will feel right.

Sometimes the space in the room is crammed with medical equipment: multiple walkers, a wheelchair, torpedo-like oxygen tanks standing in a corner, the shrill whooshing noise of an oxygen concentrator, piles of diapers and bed pads, not to mention packages of gauze, ointments, bottles of medication, and more. Some bedrooms of the dying feel almost as institutional as a hospital room. The only thing they are missing is a monitor for vital signs beeping on the wall behind the bed.

For the space to support a different feeling, all of these things need to be removed or put out of sight. Thought should be given as to how to make sure what is needed is readily at hand but not in the immediate line of sight of the person dying or people visiting.

If the dying person is in a hospital or nursing home room, then a great deal of consideration should be given to how to make the space more like the person's room at home. That means having in view some of the objects and images that matter most to this person. That could be artwork, family photographs, wall hangings, plants, stuffed animals, electric candles, and so on. While being at home brings the comfort of having all of a person's own furniture and objects around them, the environment may still need adjusting to contain more of what matters to the person.

For example, in my home I have a number of beautiful land-scape scrolls I collected when traveling through China and Japan. They hang now in the living room. My plan would include moving at least a couple of those scrolls into the bedroom, so I could see them when I can no longer get out of bed.

A woman I worked with once was in a hospital bed in the living room of her son's two-family house. The home was split into apartments that were side by side, rather than up and down. When you went through the outside door to the house, you entered a small vestibule with two doors, one leading to the son's living space and the other to his sister's living space. The son did not have children, but his sister had two young ones.

During the time I worked with the dying woman on meaning, legacy, and planning, her grandchildren from next door would often wander into the room and play quietly or draw pictures at a small table.

At one point, the dying woman asked her son to hang the pictures her grandchildren had just made. From then on, every time the children were around, they painted pictures that their uncle or mother hung on the walls around the room. This activity continued through the entire vigil. By the time this woman died, the walls were covered with her grandchildren's paintings, like an exhibit of primitive art. The drawings were always filled with bright colors and happy scenes, which made the whole room feel festive, even in the darker moments of her labored breathing.

We are so conditioned not to think about choices, that some considerations never even occur to us. It took years of my working with the dying to first think about where the bed is in the room and what the person lying in it sees in front of them. Now those considerations seem so obvious to me. A doula will also raise the question about what should be in the line of sight in all directions, and how easy it is to access various parts of the bed. One good way to think about these things is to have a family member, friend, or the doula lie down in the bed and look around the room to see what the dying person sees from their vantage point.

When Jerry was dying, his bed was in a small bedroom in his daughter's home. He had lived there for eight years before he was diagnosed with lung cancer. The room had two windows side by side on one wall and another window on the wall at a right angle to that. Jerry's bed was against an inside wall facing the wall with the one window. To the right of the single window was a large, built-in desk with shelves above it. Most of the other wall space was taken up by a closet and small bathroom. So the only wall they could hang pictures on was behind the bed.

Jerry enjoyed seeing the tree limbs and leaves through the windows, but the light didn't penetrate very far into the room. The window curtains and the hill behind the house blocked the sun much of the day. The side of the room with his bed felt dark and colder in the early spring of his dying. From the time he had first moved in, he had never liked the arrangement of this room.

He chose not to tell his daughter because it was her home, and he didn't want to offend her.

Now that he was bedbound, the position of the bed made him feel disconnected from the outside; even though he could see trees, he was far from the windows. Also, there wasn't any wall space to hang pictures of his family, which he wanted to look at as much as he could. It took some conversation about the feeling in the room and what he wanted to be looking at, before they decided to change the room around.

They moved the bed so the head of it was just below the double windows. This way, during the day, natural light poured onto his bed in waves of warmth. Since it was spring, they could also open the windows to allow in the fresh air, tinged with the scent of pine and the sounds of the birds calling to each other through the day. At night he was serenaded by the pulsing croaks of frogs in a nearby patch of wetland.

When he was propped up well with pillows, Jerry could tilt his head back and look out the double windows into the sky. He felt like he was almost outside. Since he was also closer to the other window, he could see the low bulky hill behind the house and watch the sun set beyond the fuzz of trees at the top of the ridge line.

Weeks after the room had been rearranged, Jerry told his daughter and the doula that watching the sky change every evening had inspired a deeper spiritual understanding in him.

"When the sunset smears the sky with intense red and orange colors, broken only by the last streaks of aqua, green, and blue, I feel like I'm with God. I fill my eyes with sky as it continues to change and grow grey until the night takes over. Then stars pop out, tiny pinpoints of light millions of years old, shining in the blackness." Jerry went on to explain that the display he watched in the day and night sky, repeating day after day with all the variations, helped him to realize that light and dark, life and death are just alternating aspects of ongoing existence. "I'm so much more at peace."

After the bed was moved, Jerry also had his son-in-law hang pictures of the family all over the wall where the bed had been. If he wasn't staring out the windows, Jerry would focus on the pictures of his family, seeing the reflection of his wife in some of the faces and recognizing what a good job they had done in raising their children and passing on their values. Their children were all happy and doing well. What greater legacy could he leave behind. The simple act of moving the bed had completely shifted his perspective, dramatically improved his quality of life, and helped him to discover a deeper part of himself. If the plan accomplished nothing more, this was enough.

The placement of the bed in a dying person's room may also satisfy cultural or religious imperatives. For example, some Jews believe that the person's feet—and therefore the foot of the bed—should point to the door of the room. Muslims believe that the person should face Mecca, which in the northeast part of the US means facing southeast but mostly east. Some people position the bed in a direction that is personally significant; for example, toward the location of their birth or toward a favorite part of the world.

This symbolic gesture, along with others, can build a cumulative sense of sacredness in the room. Sometimes the dying person's bed is moved into the center of a room so that people can get all around it to hold hands in a ritual conducted each morning or evening of a vigil or right after the last breath.

Another consideration regarding the room is its overall appearance. Some people need the space uncluttered, making it feel more "Zen-like"; others want to move collectibles, artwork, plants—the things they love—into the room, because they appreciate the fullness of having all of that stuff around them.

Entering the Space

At the time a person is actively dying, they are usually unresponsive. Many people assume that unresponsive means unaware. But my experience with dying people suggests that hearing is the last of the senses to go. So, while the dying person may be deep inside and not have the energy to put forth a response, they probably hear everything. That means that people should say only those things they would say if the person were awake and alert.

Beyond hearing, it is also quite possible that levels of awareness we don't know much about are still operating, and the person knows what is happening around them. For these reasons, caregivers and visitors to the bedside should be thoughtful and caring about what they say and do in the dying room and the space immediately outside it. This isn't the place for casual talk about what happened during the day, world news, or the difficulties at work. It is a place to share in a deep way and to have meaningful conversation.

Some normal talk is still acceptable, even desired, but it should be brief or taken elsewhere—unless the dying person has specifically asked the family to keep things normal and wants everyday talk in their room.

Even the mental energy that people carry into the space has an impact on how the space feels to the person dying and to the caregivers that spend hours at a time there. If a person is caught up in anger over some event, like traffic on the way to the visit or trouble in a relationship at home, they will bring that mental energy into the room. Like an odorless, invisible gas, it will spread across the space, even though the feeling isn't expressed verbally.

People's everyday minds are filled with the debris of past events—the confused jumble of half-thought-out ideas, wishes about the future, or emotions—that overlay mental activity with a charged energy. All that affects the space. It's important to enter the dying room in a clear-minded way that is more conducive to maintaining a sense of the sacred around the bedside.

There are many ways to prepare people to enter the dying space in a more mindful way. For example, people might be requested to take off their shoes just before entering the room. The act of removing one's shoes signals that the space they will enter isn't an ordinary space. When we enter holy places in the world, a temple or mosque, for example, we acknowledge that we're connecting to something special by covering or uncovering our heads, taking off our shoes, or gesturing in a special way. Any ritual act like that prepares us to leave behind everyday concerns and thoughts—to open to something deeper. That is a good way to bring a greater sense of how special this event is into the room and to the bedside of the dying.

Celia was a woman in her sixties, dying from lung cancer. She really appreciated the idea of changing people's mind state before they entered the room during her last days. As she thought about this and discussed it with the doula, Celia recognized that the feeling she wanted people to have as they entered her room was gratitude.

She had come from very impoverished circumstances, growing up in Croatia. She emigrated to the United States in her early twenties and managed to go to college by working full time and attending school at night. Throughout her life, she felt grateful for everything she was able to achieve, for the friends she loved, and for the life of comfort she was able to have in the United States. She couldn't understand how so many people lived lives of privilege yet still felt so ungrateful for what they had.

Although she never married or had children, her friendships were incredibly close and deep. She became the favorite "aunt" to many of her friends' children. As the doula and Celia discussed the meaning in her life and planned her legacy project, gratitude was a central value and a focus of that work. Celia's main legacy was helping people to feel grateful and recognizing how that led to happiness. She particularly wanted to pass this message on to all her "nieces" and "nephews."

With the doula's help, she created a life scroll that gave top billing to the two values Celia felt defined her life: gratitude and purpose. Celia wanted the scroll to travel between her friends' homes after she died, so that their children could see her legacy and be reminded of its messages.

When the doula and Celia finally planned how people should enter her room, Celia knew that she wanted to incorporate a feeling of gratitude. She didn't want people to be sad around her because she was dying and they would miss her. Gratitude, she felt, was bigger than loss.

On Celia's initiative, a favorite chair from the living room was placed at the entrance to her bedroom. The chair had a high back, no arms, and a wide seat; it was comfortable yet also very supportive. It was covered with fabric she loved that she had purchased on one of her trips to Eastern Europe.

The doula wrote a simple sign that she attached to the doorframe of Celia's room, right next to the chair. It read: "Please sit here for a few moments before entering my room. Connect to a feeling of gratitude for all we have shared together or what we will share in the next several moments."

At times during the vigil for Celia, three or four people would come at the same time to visit. But each one took a turn sitting on the chair before entering Celia's room. Even her friends' young children sat on the chair and tried to follow Celia's request. Everyone talked about the special feeling in the room, a reverence that seemed to hang in the air and soothe their hearts.

Light and Smell

The plan for the last days of life should also consider the quality of the light in the room and the fragrance in the air. These elements can affect mood, bring greater comfort, deepen awareness, and serve to enhance the atmosphere in the room.

Each dying person thinks about these elements in their own way. Take light, for example. Some people love having natural light flood the room during the daytime. Like cats, they soak it up and relish the warmth. Other people may want sheer material placed over the windows to diffuse the light as it enters, making it feel more gentle. Still others may want more opaque shades drawn, maintaining a subdued light in the room even at the brightest times of day.

At night, some people want the intimate light from a table lamp or a tall standing lamp, rather than a harsh overhead light. Lampshades can also be covered with cloth to change the color or texture of the light. I understood the role of light for the first time when a dying person I worked with placed a turquoise-blue scarf over the lamp at the side of her bed. The soft-colored light it generated filtered onto that side of the bed and the chair I was sitting on. The light made me feel peaceful and serene. It seemed to have that same effect on her.

Candles can create a very warm, cozy light in a room, as can the soft white string lights people use at holidays. One person I worked with strung chains of tiny red lights on the molding at the top of the walls all around the room. It made the room feel warm and added a playful, almost cheerful atmosphere.

Like light, fragrance can alter the feeling in a room. The sense of smell is perhaps the strongest of all the senses. Most people have had the experience of catching a particular smell in the air and immediately recalling an event or emotion connected to that smell. Every time I'm around the smell of warm or baking corn bread, I go back to one of my fondest childhood memories: walking with my mother up the block from the bakery toward our apartment building, sharing a slice of warm, freshly baked corn bread. The feelings of love and home come back to me in such a palpable way. Similar to how I felt when my mother or father would read to me before bed each night.

For many people, the smell of something baking has that same effect. So part of a vigil plan could include periodically warming bread or cookies in the oven to spread that aroma to the room where the person is dying.

Scented candles, diffusers, incense, essential oils—all of these methods of filling a room with fragrance can play a useful role in the vigil plan. Besides the emotional comfort of many fragrances, the smell can cover other, less-pleasant odors that are often part of the dying process.

I once worked with a Buddhist man who requested that he not be moved for three days after his death to let his spirit fully depart from the area around his body. To ensure that the odor of beginning decay wouldn't fill the room, we decided to burn incense day and night. He had been in the habit of burning sandalwood incense at his personal alter every morning for decades. His altar was in the room where he planned to die. Even the walls and furniture had absorbed the scent of sandalwood. You could always smell it, although sometimes it was faint, like a distant memory.

For the three days after his death, his wife burned incense around the clock. When I went back to conduct the brief ritual he and I had discussed, I didn't smell anything other than sandalwood. Later, when I reprocessed the dying experience with his wife, she told me that every time she went in the room to burn another stick of incense, she felt her husband's spirit. She imagined his essence, like the essence of the incense, present but unseen, lingering around the bed. Although she herself was not Buddhist, she decided to continue burning incense every morning for forty days after his body was taken, to honor him and his beliefs. Forty days is approximately the time some Buddhists believe the spirit needs to traverse the world between this life and the next.

Sound

We connect to music and sound at a very deep level of our being. We listen to it in quiet moments for the pure enjoyment it brings; it accompanies us as we drive, when we stand in an elevator or walk through the mall. It uplifts us in church, inspires us deeply in concert halls, gets us moving on the dance floor, and helps us fall asleep at night. It is part of almost every special human event, from the Olympics to weddings, graduations, dinner parties, parades, and an endless list of other occasions.

Every culture around the world, all the way back to the furthest reaches of prehistory, has had music. It is widely believed that some kind of systematic use of sound or music predates speech and was probably used to communicate. It may even predate humans, originating in the animal kingdom.

On a personal level, we know that the music we love is part of our identity. Whether it's classical, gospel, rap, bebop, show tunes, jazz—we feel a special connection to particular music in a way that helps us to define who we are. Recent work with Alzheimer's patients has demonstrated that individualized playlists of music they love—particularly from their teen years when adult identities are formed—can reach beyond their dementia to allow better engagement with the world around them and an improved sense of well-being.

As has been stated earlier, we know that hearing is the last of the senses to go as a person is dying. I have seen a dying person respond—to their name, a song, or the playing of an instrument at the bedside—right up to moments before they died, long after they stopped seeing, feeling, or smelling. Research using electroencephalograms of people's brain waves has proven that people hear until the moment of death.

One of the reasons for the primacy of hearing is that the brain processes sound five times faster than visual imagery. So while light is almost a million times faster than sound, hearing is faster than seeing. We are built this way because hearing was vital to staying alive in the jungles and savannahs our ancestors roamed. In the darkness of night, we can't see well, but we can hear sounds of approaching predators.

Every vigil plan should include the type of music the dying person wants to hear, right down to particular pieces, songs, and musicians. Doulas make sure that music is readily available to play at any time during the vigil.

In some vigils, the dying person has requested that music be played all the time—sometimes more quietly than at other times—depending on what else is happening at the moment. In other vigils, the time to play music is up to the discretion of the family or the doula. Sometimes a person may ask that no music be played during the final hours to moments of life. But I have also seen a person completely relax into letting go of their bodies when a particular piece of music is played in combination with guided imagery.

One of the most magical moments I can recall occurred when a doula sang a particular song to a man in excruciating pain. John was in his early sixties, dying from pancreatic cancer, which can be incredibly painful. He received extremely high doses of morphine intravenously, but still his pain wasn't well managed.

All day and through much of the night, John's wife, Cathy, went in and out of the bedroom where he was dying. But she never stayed at his bedside for more than fifteen minutes or so, because she couldn't stand watching his body wracked by pain. Seeing someone you love suffer in this way can feel unusually cruel. Cathy repeated many times how "unfair" it seemed to her. She said that John was one of the most generous and good-hearted people she had ever known.

"Why would someone like him die so miserably?" she would ask. She didn't really expect an answer to that question. Each of the doulas who attended the vigil responded in a way that acknowledged how hard it was to watch someone you love die in pain, then rub her upper back or give her a hug.

Doulas had been doing vigil work for three days when this special moment occurred. They had used guided visualization to try to help ease his pain—but it hadn't seemed to have much effect. They avoided touch out of fear that even light physical sensations might increase his pain. Occasionally, a doula might slip their hand underneath his hand to let him know they were there alongside him.

On the night before he died, a doula who hadn't been at the vigil before came for a shift that was due to end at midnight.

Grace had a beautiful voice and loved to sing to a dying person during her vigil shifts. Before arriving, she had prepared for her shift by searching on her computer for ballads and folk music to sing. Grace knew from the vigil plan that this was the type of music John liked. One of the songs that came up in her search was Leonard Cohen's "Hallelujah," which she knew and loved.

Grace started her shift by talking with the doula she was replacing to find out what had happened during the hours before she arrived. Then Grace talked to Cathy to see how she was doing. They spoke at the entrance to the bedroom so Grace could keep her eyes on John. Even though he wasn't making any sounds, Grace could see the pain tightening his body, an unchanging grimace frozen on his face.

"I can't bear to watch this," Cathy said. "I try to stay close to the bedroom, but I can only go in for a few minutes at a time. It has been worse than it is now, believe it or not. But it's still excruciating to watch."

"It's so hard to see someone you love in this kind of pain," Grace responded. "I'll be here for hours, so we can talk more at any point that you want to. I'm also going to sing to him periodically, which I've seen ease people's pain."

Cathy went off to a study next door to the bedroom, where she had placed a cot to get sleep when she could. Grace went in to sit at the bedside next to John. On the other side of the bed, a privately hired home health aide sat, pressing the rescue button on the morphine every minute or two.

After sitting for a while, Grace picked up the guitar she had brought with her. She hadn't decided in advance which songs she would play or in what order. She liked to just allow the feeling of the moment to call forth the song. She heard the echo of Leonard Cohen's gruff voice singing "Hallelujah" in her mind. She started to play the notes softly to see how John would react. She felt rather than saw the slightest loosening of the muscles in his face. The home health aide said, "He likes that." So Grace began to sing, quietly at first, then let her voice carry more of the passion in the song as John seemed to relax more and incline his head a touch in her direction.

A few bars into the song, Cathy came into the room and joined in singing the song. Grace later said that the room seemed to fill with the energy of the song and their two voices. It felt to her as if John was singing inside as well, his body visibly in less pain.

When the song was done, Cathy grabbed Grace's hand and held it firmly between her hands, clearly moved by the last few minutes of song. "That's the first time in days that he has looked calm," Cathy said.

The home health aide agreed. "I haven't had to push the rescue button since you started singing," she said.

Still holding Grace's hand, Cathy asked her, "Why did you sing that song?"

"It was the first one that came to mind as I sat here," Grace said. She thought Cathy had asked that question because of how peaceful John seemed now. The grimace that had seemed permanent on his face was gone. Grace was stunned by the next thing Cathy said.

"That was our wedding song."

Tears ran down Cathy's face. Grace also welled up, recognizing the magic of what had just happened. Cathy asked if they could sing the song again. As they did, Cathy knelt at the side of the bed and ever so gently caressed John's arm. When they were done, no one spoke. They all just absorbed the feeling of light and warmth in the room. John's whole body had relaxed. Cathy stayed next to John for well over an hour, the longest time she had been in the room since the vigil had started.

John's pain did come back in the later hours of Grace's shift. But it was never as bad as it had been. She sang "Hallelujah" a couple more times, along with other songs. Every time Grace sang, John relaxed. When the next doula arrived, Grace stayed long enough to give her a report and sing "Hallelujah" one last time. Cathy had come in to just sit at the bedside and listen. Then Grace told John she was leaving.

Cathy walked Grace to the doorway of the bedroom and hugged her for a long time. "I will never forget what you did," Cathy said. "You have the right name. You gave me something to remember and hold on to with joy in the midst of all the suffering I have had to watch. Not only did you ease John's pain but mine as well. Thank you."

The doulas who followed Grace said that John stayed peaceful for the remaining eight hours of his life. In the last couple of hours, his pain seemed to vanish altogether.

Cathy was so touched by the coincidence of Grace singing her and John's wedding song that she had the song played at John's funeral. It was the only music played. Everyone in the room cried when Cathy told the story of the night Grace sang the song without knowing its significance in advance.

Later, during the visit to reprocess the vigil, Cathy said that hearing Grace sing "Hallelujah" was a turning point for her. It allowed her to touch again the joy of being with John. It gave her something positive to hang on to whenever the anguish of his dying surged through her.

This story shows how powerful music or sound can be for both the dying person and the family. Doulas have had every type of music requested for a vigil, from Gregorian chant to Thelonious Monk, from Frank Sinatra to the Grateful Dead.

Some people prefer hearing recordings of nature sounds: a stream meandering through a forest, chattering around and over rocks that line its path; a waterfall tumbling into a frothy pool; a summer rainstorm slashing its way across a corn field, thunder rumbling in the distance; the gentle swishing sound of waves as they roll over a sandy shore, then get sucked back out to a vast ocean; or birds calling excitedly to one another at the edges of a meadow. Using the kind of music or sound the person loves, at times combining it with visualization and ritual, can be a very effective.

Readings

Reading to a dying person may also help them to relax and put them in touch with the spiritual dimension of their being. Many people want passages of scripture, the Psalms, or other spiritual material read to them. It may remind them of beliefs they hold about the dying experience and what happens afterward. This can reassure a person as the approach of the unknown looms larger and larger. It may also help the person to hold on to the values and beliefs that have guided them in life and that they believe will still serve them in dying, at the moment of death, and during what may lay beyond this life.

Naturally, as with the other choices a person makes in creating a plan, readings should reflect the kind of material that matters most to them. If it isn't scripture or spiritual texts of some kind, then it may be poetry, a favorite novel that they read over and over again throughout their life, special-occasion cards they exchanged with loved ones, the stories of their life collected in a memory book, a journal, or other form of legacy.

Just hearing the singsong sound of the human voice reading out loud can soothe and reassure. Even if the dying person can't hold on to the exact meaning of the words, the rhythm, tone, and emotion the reader uses will convey comforting messages.

On rare occasions, the dying person may prefer silence in the last hours or minutes of life. No music and no readings. Sharon was one of those people.

Sharon had lived a reclusive, quiet life—never married nor had children. At the end of her life, she reluctantly agreed to have a niece take care of her so that she could stay out of a nursing home. Sharon saw the value in having doulas to support her niece. However, she thought that music or readings would feel irritating and disruptive as she prepared internally to die.

She requested that only one person be in the room at a time—either her niece or a doula. She also asked that no one play music or watch TV in the rooms close to her bedroom—to avoid having some of the sound leak into her dying space. The doulas honored and supported Sharon's choices about music and reading out of the fundamental doula belief that each person is entitled to decide what their dying experience should look like and sound like.

Touch and Holding

Continuing to touch a person who is dying is quite important. Unfortunately, many people avoid touching the dying, because they are afraid to hurt their skin or body in some way. Of course one needs to be gentle with someone who is in a fragile physical condition, but touch is a basic human need. Touch offers connection and helps create intimacy. It can encourage a person to continue to struggle with a deep question or reassure them that they have the strength to face a difficult next step. It lets a dying person know—in a very direct way—that someone is there at the bedside, willing to accompany them in their process of dying.

Doulas will ask about cultural norms around touch. In some communities, like those of Orthodox Jews or Muslims, it would be wrong for a man to touch a dying woman if they weren't close relatives; the same would apply for a female doula touching an Orthodox man. Of course touch is very personal, and some people want to be touched only in particular ways. I have known a number of people who didn't want their feet touched or massaged, for example.

As Claire was getting close to actively dying, her husband asked the hospice team if she could be placed in a facility for a few days of respite care, so he could recover his energy before the physical and emotional demands of a vigil. In hospice, a family is entitled to request up to five days of respite. They usually make such a request when they cannot continue to care for the person without a break, or because they have a commitment to a family or work event that will take them away for several days.

Claire went to a hospice facility. After only a couple of days there, she suddenly declined and became unresponsive. The floor nurse had called me to say she thought it was time to start the vigil. Claire's vital signs had dropped, and her breathing had slowed down. I went to visit her that evening to confirm what the nurse had seen earlier. Sometimes people decline and appear on the cusp of actively dying, but then stabilize and stay at a plateau for days.

Claire was only in her fifties and had been eating up to the night before. Her heart was in good shape—she had stomach cancer—and she had enough body mass to sustain her for a while without eating. So it was possible that the vigil wasn't needed yet.

When I arrived at Claire's room, her sister and her sister's husband were there, along with her mother and an adult niece. I had met Claire and her husband previously, but this was the first time I was meeting other members of the family. I introduced myself and spent a few minutes explaining the doula approach to them.

Then Claire's sister asked me the question I get asked all the time: How long did I think Claire had? I couldn't see Claire's face or the front of her body, because she was turned to face away from where I was standing. But I was able to go around the bed and kneel down in front of her. I spoke gently to Claire, telling her I was there and that I was going to look at her hands and watch her breathing. I also told her that I was going to place my hand on her arm. As I did that, lightly caressing her arm, her mother, who was standing at the foot of the bed, said, "Ooh, I wanted to do that, but I was afraid to."

Even before I continued to assess Claire further, I told her mother to come over to where I was and caress her daughter, taking my place. After she had spent some time caressing her daughter, I went back to assessing how Claire was. I thought the nurse was correct in her earlier assessment, so I told the family that my visit would mark the start of the vigil. I then called the doula who was signed up to take the next shift so that she would know we were starting.

The doula approach encourages touch by directly suggesting it or modeling how to hold a loved one's hand and caress their arms, feet, face, and head. When appropriate—especially if discussed ahead of time with the dying person—family and friends should feel free to climb in bed, lie alongside the dying person, even snuggle up to them.

Just as I had learned when I took a birth doula class, we teach adult children, a spouse, or parents of a dying child to get in bed behind the dying person and hold them between their legs, the dying person's back up against their chest. In this position, they can support and encircle the dying person with their whole body. This form of loving embrace is extremely comforting for both people.

The Written Plan

The final outcome of exploring and discussing all the aspects of the environment and atmosphere around a dying person is either an informal understanding of what the person wants or a written plan. Writing down a plan gives clearer direction to everyone involved in the care. But the plan is simply an outline; it isn't a rigid document that people must cling to. Every vigil will deviate from the plan. It has to. The dying process may be predictable in general but not in the lived details of the moment-to-moment way it unfolds.

The dying process always offers surprises in the way a particular person's body breaks down and in the thoughts and feelings the family experiences. As the plan and the reality of the process intersect, the doula approach is to remain flexible and support people in a way that is right for them in that moment, without judging their responses or actions and without imposing any ideas of what should happen.

Earlier in this chapter, I introduced an aspect of Celia's vigil plan: her request that people sit on a chair and connect to a feeling of gratitude before they entered her room. That was the first element of her plan as it was written down. Here is the rest of Celia's plan, to demonstrate what a full plan might look like:

- Tell me stories of our times together; address any unfinished business; or just speak from the heart.

- Spray lavender essential oils on my sheets and pillows each day.

- Read to me from the poetry books on my night table.

- Play the Bach Cantatas or the nature sounds CD called *Peaceful Forest.*

- Guide me in the visualization of the Plitvice Lakes National Forest in Croatia with its series of cascading lakes and waterfalls that I love.

- Add to my life scroll how you will carry me in your heart, so those who read it in the future may be inspired to do the same thing.

- Whoever feels comfortable can lie with me, hold my hand, or caress my arms, head, and face.

- Place the small statues of bears I have collected over the years on all the surfaces in the room and especially near the bed.

- Right after I die, let the doula guide people who want to help wash my body, comb my hair, and clothe my body in the silk blouse and skirt I have chosen for that time.

- Read my life scroll and unfurl it on top of me until my body is taken.

- Allow time before the funeral home people come, so those gathered can tell favorite stories, then toast those experiences and special moments with the Grasevina wine from Croatia I put aside for this purpose.

Celia's plan incorporates all the different aspects of what a plan may include. It is possible to feel her personality in the details; even as she specifies the things that will help her be more comfortable or deepen the experience of sacredness, she is also taking care of the people at her bedside.

Celia died very peacefully. Her breathing slowed down, becoming quieter and more shallow, until it seemed to disappear the way a snowflake disappears on warm earth at the very start of winter: visible one moment in its delicate beauty, then just gone, leaving behind a hint of glistening wetness to let you know it was there the moment before.

Celia's friends felt privileged to wash her body afterward. When they drank her Croatian wine, it was in the spirit of celebration, in the spirit of gratitude that was so important to Celia. In the end, they promised one another to honor Celia's wish to have her life scroll travel to each of their homes for six months at a time. And they promised to keep speaking about the example of her life and death to their children.

CHAPTER 9

Guided Imagery

You use your ability to visualize images in your mind every day—even without those images being tied to immediate external stimuli. When you remember a past event or use your imagination to picture something that hasn't happened yet, you are, of course, using your ability to visualize.

Think about the last time you pictured someone's face in your mind, as you thought of calling them on the phone or imagined them sitting at their desk in the office. Think about how you envision a curve in the road ahead when you drive home at night or see yourself sitting in a hot bath after you get home. Just for a moment, imagine soaring like a bird in an updraft of wind, lifting off the dusty, brown prairie, a cushion of air beneath your outstretched wings, feeling the exhilaration of being carried ever higher without effort. You can see and feel these images because of your capacity to visualize.

In a sense, what you just did was use guided imagery to experience an event that wasn't actually happening at that moment—except in your mind. To arrive at a particular outcome, athletes use guided imagery to map out every step or movement in an event or race. They do it many times, until they easily see it happening in precisely the way they envision it. As they guide their imagination in this way, they make it much more likely that the real event will happen the way they pictured it.

People can learn a new technique simply by envisioning how to do it in their mind. A surgeon might practice a tricky new surgical technique in her mind; a composer might hear in his mind how adding a different instrument would change the overall sound of a symphony he is writing—without that instrument, or any others, being in the room.

The reason that practicing in your imagination works is that the brain processes the images and feelings as if they were actually occurring in the outside world. When you get really good at the technique of guiding your mind into particular images, your body and brain won't be able to tell the imagined from the real. Remember the last time you woke up in the middle of a vivid dream? It felt completely real, and you reacted to it in the way you would if it had been happening out in the world—but it was only a story playing out across the ephemeral ground of your imagination.

Guided imagery can be used in a great many ways at the end of life. It can help in exploring meaning and imagining a legacy project; in envisioning how the dying person wants the environment to look and sound; in managing physical and emotional symptoms; in cultivating a general sense of well-being; in preparing to let go of the body with less fear and greater acceptance; and in dealing with spiritual distress. It can also be used to offer love, seek forgiveness, bring closure to old wounds or broken relationships, clear one's mind, bring greater focus to an activity, deepen the experience of ritual, and help heal the devastating feelings of loss that follow death.

What makes this tool particularly useful in doula work is that it gives a dying person and the family greater control over what happens in the dying process. As physical symptoms worsen, guided imagery can help alleviate them. When a dying person wakes up in the middle of the night and struggles with fear or anxiety about what lies ahead, guided imagery is a technique to help them let go of those emotions and get back to sleep. Even when a person is unresponsive in the last days of life, I believe that guiding them with appropriate images helps them to feel more comfortable, safe, and accepting of the internal journey toward death.

When a person uses guided imagery, they enter an altered state of mind. There are similarities to other altered states, such as hypnosis, deep meditation, and waking dream. While it is possible to use this technique on oneself—and I do that in my life all the time—it has greater power when another person is doing the guiding. Then the person being guided can relax and allow the guide to prompt the images. When the guide is good, the images will flow through the person being guided almost as if they were really occurring to them.

While it is certainly true that guided imagery works best when conducted by someone with experience, it is a very forgiving technique. Just by virtue of the fact that a person being guided surrenders themselves to an altered internal state, the stumbles, misspoken words, or poor pacing of an inexperienced guide won't totally break the spell of a visualization.

In classes I teach to train people in this technique, the universal experience is that even a first-timer can be successful in guiding another person inward. This is not to say that a person shouldn't practice guiding—they should. And they will get better, become more effective, and be able to try out new approaches. But performance anxiety shouldn't get in the way of supporting someone through guided imagery. The benefits of this technique are too clear to hesitate in using it.

Death Visualization

I started my first meeting with Julie and her sister Estelle by giving them a brief introduction to the doula approach. Before going further, I asked them if there were any pressing issues they wanted to discuss. Julie was in her late seventies and had cancer. She said that recently she had been having panic attacks, which she had never had before. A feeling of terror would suddenly overtake her; she would sweat profusely, her heart would race, and she would have trouble breathing.

I asked her to try to go back in her memory to the first time she remembered having an attack. Her sister Estelle said it had been three weeks earlier, right after the nurse's visit that day. With that, Estelle put it together. "Jules, remember, that was the day the nurse went over the signs and symptoms of dying."

What Julie realized in further discussion was that she had a primal fear of dying—of the process itself—in spite of her belief that her soul would go to heaven. I suggested that she talk to the nurse about the panic attacks and ask about medication that might help during a severe attack. Then I taught Julie a breath relaxation technique that might stop an attack if she used it at the first signs or ease the severity once an attack was underway. I also suggested that we create a guided visualization she could use to address the underlying fear of dying.

At my next visit, I asked Julie what she believed happened internally as a person died. She told me that she had read many accounts of near-death experiences and believed that they were real. "Three things seemed to occur in many of those accounts," she told me. "A dark tunnel, a beautiful white or golden light, and meeting the spirits of those who died before."

I had Julie close her eyes and imagine that experience in as much detail as possible, using all her senses. I wrote down the essence of what she said, paying special attention to some of the exact words she used. I later wove all the images together into a narrative. During the next visit, we spent part of the time trying out a visualization based on the imagery she had given me. At the heart of the visualization, it went something like this:

You are feeling a great sense of peace in a vast space with no form and no objects. In front of you the space coalesces into a dark tunnel that seems to draw you forward. As you enter the tunnel, the darkness feels warm and comforting. Its walls are not hard like rock but soft and seem to hum with energy. The air in the tunnel has the woody, sweet yet slightly spicy fragrance of frankincense, which adds to the sense of peace and holiness in the tunnel. You travel through this tunnel at great speed, but somehow that feels comforting and safe.

Then you become aware that there is an end to the tunnel that appears to be an intense white light. As you reach it, the light pulls you forward. Now you see that what appeared white is actually a whole range of subtle hues from milky white to pink and gold, like being inside a pearl that has no boundaries. The light seems to shimmer with a vibrant energy that fills you with an incredible sense of joy. Its essence is love magnified to a fullness you could never have imagined.

If anything, you are moving faster now through this exquisite light energy. You begin to realize that you aren't alone in the light. You sense the presence of spirits of loved ones who have died before you. They appear as figures of light within the light, but you know who each one is. You can feel their love and welcome as you proceed through the light. You know you will soon join them and become part of this vibrant other-worldly energy beyond your current life. And this feels right and good to you.

You know there is nothing to fear in death because of the beauty and love that await you there. Even if you don't completely let go into this light right now, you know that one day soon you will, seeing its incredible beauty and feeling the joy that fills you now. You will soon surrender completely to the light and move onward through it into the next realm of existence.

Julie liked the visualization and began using it for herself later that day. I made her a recording of it so that she could relax and have my voice guide her whenever she wanted. Over the next several weeks, the panic attacks subsided. Julie continued to listen to the visualization every day. At some point, she said that the visualization had become so familiar that she could close her eyes, picture the tunnel, and move immediately into the pearlescent light that filled her with peace and joy.

By the time death was drawing near, Julie no longer had panic attacks. She told me that she was beginning to look forward to death, curious to see if, in fact, her experience would match the visualization. When the vigil began, Julie was unresponsive. The people who attended her vigil continued to speak the visualization to her or use the recording of it multiple times a day. Right after Julie's last breath, a smile broke out on her face. Estelle said she was sure that smile meant Julie had entered the light she had seen each day in her visualization.

The doula approach promotes a very direct engagement with the process of dying. Julie's visualization actualized that engagement and allowed her and the family to bring a sense of sacredness into the experience. The visualization was her story of how she thought the dying process would unfold. But it was also an expression of what she saw as the deepest truth of dying.

By doing the visualization over and over again—and being guided with it while she was actively dying—she gave herself the opportunity to arrive at a deep acceptance of death. I believe it also allowed her to let go of her body peacefully when the time came. The ease and dignity of her dying meant a great deal to Estelle and the rest of the family.

Whenever a person creates a death visualization, it should reflect their beliefs and understanding of what happens in the dying process. Whether the person is Christian or Jewish, Buddhist, Muslim, or atheist, the story needs to conform to their truth about dying. Everyone has a story about death. Grappling with that story helps the person find a framework for the experience and reach some level of acceptance.

A Special Place

Another kind of guided imagery that helps people lessen anxiety and bring them a greater sense of well-being is what I call a "Special Place" visualization. It uses the images of a place in nature that is special to the person and helps them connect to feelings of peace and tranquillity. It may also connect a person to feeling close to something larger than themselves—a presence or force that animates nature or the universe—whether you call that presence God, Oneness, a Higher Power, Goodness, or the Ground of Being.

The visualization uses all the senses to help the person feel they are really there. Then they can absorb the beauty and peace of the place and hold on to those feelings inside themselves after the visualization has ended. In this way, they may achieve a greater overall sense of well-being and gain the strength to deal with the symptoms and the dying process in the days ahead.

The person might select a place they know well or one they know only from a picture in a magazine or online. They might even create an imaginary place that represents their ideal of what that kind of place would look like.

When Arthur thought about the place he wanted to use for this visualization, he immediately pictured Blue Mountain Lake in the Adirondacks. Almost every summer for quite a few years, he and his wife would vacation there, taking their children to a rustic resort that had a large central lodge and a group of cabins perched on a hillside overlooking a tiny beach and the lake. They all loved the last cabin on the hillside. It had a living room area that jutted out toward a boat dock.

"When you sat on the couch by the big picture window," Arthur said, "all you saw was the lake, as if you were sitting on the deck of a houseboat. I could spend hours just looking out at the water, a big island in the lake, and the far shore."

The family spent most of their time boating on the lake, using the kayaks, sunfish sailboats, or rowboats that the resort kept for guests. Some days Arthur would go off on his own for a few hours in one of the old wooden rowboats. He would row for a while, just to work the muscles in his arms and abdomen, to feel his strength against the resistance of the water.

Then he would lie in the bottom of the boat, using a life preserver as a pillow, and let the breeze and the current of the lake take him wherever it did. He loved the feeling of just floating along, gently rocked by the lake, listening to the water lapping against the boat's hull. He could close his eyes and let his mind drift like the boat or stare up at the blue sky and watch the clouds floating above him. Sometimes he would imagine shapes in the clouds, just as he had when he was a child, seeing a galloping horse or an elephant with a very long trunk. He remembered those moments of drifting on the lake as some of the most peaceful in his life.

So floating on the lake became his special-place visualization. It started with watching himself walk out onto the dock to untether the boat and the feeling in his arms as he set out rowing across the lake. The imagery included the gray-green color of the water, his view of one of the large islands in the lake, and the pine forest that ran all along the lake's shoreline, punctuated occasionally by a house or dock. It included the birds he would see, the smell of pine and lake water, the robin's egg–blue sky and puffy white clouds. He could hear the sound of the oars as they splashed into the water and the squeak in the oar sockets as he swung the oars around for the next stroke.

Then he would see himself lie down in the boat and feel the incredible peace of floating, supported by the polished wooden bottom of the boat and the body of the lake, and having no need to worry about direction or arriving anywhere. He could feel the boat gently dipping and rocking with the current of the lake, as if nature itself were rocking him.

For Arthur, nature was where he felt close to something bigger than himself. He felt at peace and safe. It allowed him to feel that he could just let go into his dying process, however it occurred. Let nature take its course. Trust that all would go well. The imagery gave him great comfort and a deep feeling of well-being. The visualization would conclude with his trip back to the dock and securing the rowboat.

Sometimes, instead of the guided imagery of setting out in the rowboat, Arthur would picture himself sitting at the bay window of his cabin, overlooking the lake, mesmerized by the constant rippling motion of its surface as if it were alive, his mind empty of all thoughts, feeling totally at peace, completely at one with the lake, trees, and sky. In this imagery, he felt that the panorama and distant view gave him perspective.

Arthur used one or the other of these related visualizations every day, sometimes a number of times during the day. He particularly liked to use the visualization when he woke up in the middle of the night and his mind was filled with too much worry to go back to sleep. Focusing on the imagery helped him recover a feeling of peace, and he would usually fall asleep as he visualized.

As Arthur's illness progressed, he found that the visualization worked best when spoken to him by the doula or his wife, Pam. Although Pam had never used guided imagery before the doula taught her what to do, it turned out that she had a natural talent for it. The doula told Pam to start a session by having Arthur focus his mind on the physical sensations of his breathing in his belly or at his nostrils. Pam also learned a body scan technique that had Arthur move his mental focus up or down his whole body, letting go of any tension or tightness he felt in his face, shoulders, belly, back, or limbs.

The doula suggested that Pam close her eyes throughout the guided imagery session and picture in her mind the scene into which she guided Arthur. Pam discovered that when she did this, it allowed her to enter the same altered mental state that Arthur did, while still maintaining her ability to guide. Seeing the image herself also helped Pam find the right pacing in her verbal phrasing and the right musicality in her voice.

Sometimes, new images would come up in her mind that she incorporated into the session. Invariably, when she later talked about these unplanned images with Arthur, she found out that they felt exactly right to him at that moment.

Not everyone can picture images clearly in their mind, but Pam had a very visual imagination that made it easier for her to guide. Arthur's ability to visualize was good, but for him it was more about the feelings the images engendered. The more times the visualization is used, the more quickly and easily the person can go there in their mind.

As Pam used the visualization more, she realized that she was getting as much out of it as Arthur. Even though the imagery was what he had chosen, she found it profoundly peaceful. The feeling she had inside after the visualization lasted for hours. She loved the idea that she could do something more for Arthur than feeding him medications and fluffing his pillows. She also gained greater confidence in her care of Arthur.

After a while, Pam created a special-place visualization for herself. There was a place along a stream that she had gone to many years earlier when she was in college. She liked to lie on a large rock that sat at a wider part of the stream. The break in the tree canopy at that spot allowed the sunlight to pour through and warm her body. Whenever she felt stressed by her studies or upcoming exams, she would go to the rock and let the sound of the rushing stream wash away her anxiety.

She pictured it now in her visualization: the sound of the stream, the light on her body, and the musky smell of the forest floor all merged together in a feeling of oneness. Just as she could capture this in her imagination and feel herself there in her mind, she knew she would be able to visualize Arthur in her mind forever, calling him back to her whenever she wanted to be with him. This thought gave her a lot of comfort.

Alleviating Physical Symptoms

Symptom relief is an important goal for end-of-life care. The doula approach focuses on working with people at a point in their illness when the care plan shifts from cure or prolonging life to better quality of life and greater comfort. Symptoms that aren't managed well will drain mental alertness and physical energy, making it much harder to explore meaning, create legacies, plan for the last days, and live with purpose.

While a special-place visualization can be effective in helping to reduce physical symptoms—such as pain, shortness of breath, nausea, and vomiting—a different kind of visualization can address these symptoms more directly. An example of this kind of visualization I call the "Healing Pond."

In the healing-pond visualization, the person imagines that they are standing at the edge of a small pond of silvery blue water. They can feel the healing energy that exists in the water. The surface of the pond seems to shimmer with light that comes from the depths, as if the pond were glowing from the inside. The person stands still for several moments, feeling the parts of their body in pain. Then slowly they enter the water, which has a heavy, viscous feel to it, more like oil than water, as it encircles their feet and ankles. They can feel the healing quality in the water so, even if they do not have pain there, their feet and ankles feel more alive, warm, and soft.

The person slowly continues to walk deeper into the pond, stopping each time the water rises to a level where it submerges a part of the body that is in pain. Standing still for several moments at that point, they can feel the water absorbing the pain, pulling it out of their body. There is something about the viscous nature of the water that pulls the pain out of the body. The glowing energy of the water dissipates the pain so that it sinks to the bottom of the pond and into the earth.

The person will continue deeper into the pond to remove the pain from every place they feel it. If the pain is in their head, they will walk into the pond up to their neck and then dunk down, completely submerging their head for several moments. After standing back up to breathe, they can dunk down again if they need more time for the water to absorb the pain. When they are done, they walk slowly back out of the pond until they are standing again at its edge. They thank the water for taking their pain, slowly open their eyes, and return from the visualization.

Another visualization for pain uses a magical salve that comes in a special jar. The person imagines opening the jar, scooping some salve onto their fingertips, then rubbing the salve onto each painful part of their body. They use slow circular motions in a counterclockwise direction, feeling the tingling energy of the salve penetrating their skin. As the magical properties of the salve reach the center of the pain, the pain begins to lessen and finally disappears, being replaced by a warm, pleasant feeling in that part of the body.

Nausea and vomiting can be treated with either of the above two visualizations for pain just by changing the words to match the symptom. If the person were using the image of the pond, they would walk in to the point where the water covers their upper stomach, just above the solar plexus. If using the salve, the person would imagine rubbing it in over the upper stomach and solar plexus.

Another visualization for nausea and vomiting would have the person imagine that they are beneath a cascade of blue light. They would picture the light flowing over their body and penetrating down through the crown of the head. As the light moves down through the body, it pulls the nauseated feelings down with it, until those feelings move out through the feet with the light to be carried into the earth. It is important that, during the visualization, the person is sitting up or at least propped up in bed. The head must be well above the stomach so that the downward flow and gravity are aligned, which counterbalances the upward energy of nausea and vomiting.

There are visualizations for virtually every symptom a dying person might experience. There is a great deal of information available through the Internet, in books, and in examples of visualizations on CDs. The real key to using this technique for alleviating symptoms is to be creative and check that the imagery works for the person being guided.

Spiritual Distress

Spiritual distress that bends a person's beliefs or shatters their faith is not uncommon at the end of life. Many people have a notion of fairness that is turned on its head when they face their own death or that of a loved one. Sometimes it is the way a person is dying that is the issue, more than the death itself. Anger, a sense of betrayal, and abandonment are the feelings that accompany spiritual distress.

A person approaching death may struggle spiritually for other reasons as well. Guilt from the past may be so powerful that it blocks a person's ability to access their connection to spirit, to God. Or a person may feel the desire to reconnect to a faith they shed years earlier but not know how to do that. The doula approach is to explore the thoughts and feelings around an issue, but dialog and internal processing may not be enough to find the way through this distress. Guided imagery can be an effective way to work on these issues from a different vantage point.

Robert was a former Catholic priest who had given up the priesthood after fifteen years. He then went on to lead a secular life, married, and had children. Somewhere along the way, he had come to have very serious doubts about his religion, even about the existence of God. When he was diagnosed with prostate cancer that had spread to his bones and other organs, his questions about God and faith became burning issues that preoccupied much of his thinking.

As I worked with Robert on life meaning, he kept returning to questions of faith. I listened to Robert without judging him or trying to give him answers. I helped him clarify thoughts that seemed fuzzy. I knew Robert would have to find his own answers to the questions that burned in his mind and heart. After working on these questions for a while, both internally and in dialog with me, Robert arrived at a dead end. He kept repeating the same thoughts and not going anywhere. I suggested we try a visualization that might lead Robert to an encounter with a spiritual figure, such as Jesus or a favorite saint. But those spiritual figures didn't feel right to him.

Then Robert spoke about another spiritual figure he had felt close to earlier in his life. "If there is one person I could have talked to about doubts and questions like this, it would have been the priest in the church my family attended," he said. "That priest, Father Tony, was the person who inspired me to think about the priesthood in the first place, and he encouraged me when I became serious about it. But Father Tony died many years ago," Robert said, somewhat forlornly.

I told Robert that he could still speak to Father Tony, at least in his imagination, through a guided imagery session. He was willing to give it a try, so he and I discussed the visualization and agreed on a structure. At the next visit, I guided Robert inward to meet Tony in the garden behind the church of his youth.

"You and Tony have the entire afternoon for this special visit, to walk together or sit on a bench in the garden," I said to Robert as he sat on the couch in the living room. His eyes were closed, and an afghan was wrapped around his shoulders to keep him warm. I closed my eyes, too. "You can see the sun directly overhead. You will know that the visit is coming to an end when the sun sinks behind a distant hill, signaling the start of evening." I suggested that Robert catch Tony up on his life. Then I told him to speak to Tony about his spiritual doubts and ask the questions that naturally came to him in that moment.

After pausing for several minutes to allow the imaginary encounter to start unfolding inside Robert, I suggested that Tony might respond with words, gestures, or just a look in his eyes.

"What Tony conveys to you will help you to see through the dark cloud of your doubts and questions," I said. After another pause, I added, "Notice that the sun has moved further across the sky, inclining toward the distant hill but still well above it. Now you may speak to Tony more about his responses to you, ask other questions, or just spend time together walking through the garden and talking about anything that the two of you want to discuss."

When it came time to bring the visualization to an end, I told Robert that the sun had dropped behind the distant hill and the visit must end. "As you say goodbye to Tony, he may have some final words of advice or a gift to give you that will help you clarify your thoughts," I said. "You may have something to offer him in return."

After a short pause, I had Robert see Tony walking across the garden and reentering the church. Then I told Robert to let the images fade from his mind, to feel again his body sitting on the couch, feel the air on the skin of his face, and then open his eyes to return to the room. Now that my eyes were open again as well, I saw that there was a radiant smile on Robert's face. His body seemed more relaxed. For the first time in weeks, he seemed less troubled.

Robert told me that Tony had said that God didn't depend on adherences to any particular rituals or observances. He said God was inside Robert, and he could find him by just looking within. "At the moment Tony said that to me, I knew it was true; God was right there inside me," Robert said. "Out of neglect, I had forgotten how to find that place inside. All my doubts and questions fell away. They were simply gone. I immediately felt God's presence inside. The relief I felt was amazing." We discussed the visualization for a while more. I asked if Tony had given Robert a gift. "Yes, he gave me Communion," Robert said, and tears ran down his face. Robert had hugged Tony in return.

For the rest of Robert's illness, he was untroubled by doubts or questions of faith. The visualization had allowed him to reconnect to the awareness of God inside himself. Everyone around Robert felt how peaceful he had become. During the vigil, people felt joyous in sitting at the bedside.

Guided imagery is a powerful technique that the doula approach uses in so many ways. It gives control back to the dying person, as well as to the caregivers. It can be used to work with anticipatory grief and is also a wonderful tool for working through grief. In the reprocessing visits doulas do after a person dies, they remind family that guided imagery can still be very helpful.

Grief is a natural process that entails its own kind of suffering. Emotions are like a tornado that swirls inside, tossing around images from the past, fears of the future, guilt, regrets, anger at the illness—sometimes even anger at the person who died—as if they were debris pulled into a vortex of pain and deposited in a jumble in the heart. Visualization can be very effective for working through some of the deeper emotions, giving you back a sense of well-being at moments, becoming an oasis in your grief. And visualization can also help you work through unfinished business or issues of forgiveness.

CHAPTER 10

Ritual

Ritual plays an important role in our lives. It is the way we recognize the heightened importance of certain events, such as birthdays, wedding anniversaries, and holidays. It also helps us observe the transition from one reality to another, such as funeral services, mourning customs, and marriage ceremonies. Some rituals are formalized into precise actions and words, ones that have been used in exactly the same way each time the ritual has been performed—perhaps for hundreds of years. Other rituals are more informal and can vary within loose boundaries of enactment according to the personality of those involved. Rituals may also evolve over time.

What makes ritual so powerful is that it contains multiple levels of meaning in a simplified, symbolic form. Think, for example, of placing a wedding ring on the fourth finger from the thumb of the left hand. The origin of this ritual act goes all the way back to at least 3000 BC in Egypt.

The ring, then usually made of twisted hemp, was a symbol of the eternal because of its round shape. It represented a binding of one to another for all time, which is why the strands were twisted together. Those meanings are, of course, still contained in the rings given today.

The hole in the ring symbolized the doorway to the future, the transition from the reality of being single to a new reality of unity. It was placed on the fourth finger of the left hand because the ancient Egyptians believed a vein ran from this finger directly to the heart, a reminder of a deep truth about marriage: it is consecrated in the heart, not through a signed document or the exchange of property.

And there are still other implications in this act. You can see how simply placing a ring on the finger of the person you marry holds such a rich fusion of meanings.

Rituals at various points of the dying process serve the same functions as those at other important moments of life. They help capture multiple layers of meaning and allow participants to express the significance of these events in their lives. As my doula work has evolved over the last thirteen years, my use of ritual has expanded and deepened.

In a way, the plan that the dying person and the family create represents a ritual of care the participants will enact during the last days of life. To make that meaning more clear, the people involved might design a ritual that signifies the start of a vigil and declares the wishes of the dying person and the family. Such a ritual would also mark a major transition from the time of illness to the final time of dying.

The ritual doesn't have to be elaborate to be effective. It should occur as soon as possible after deciding to start the vigil—perhaps during the first shift or as soon as people can gather. The ritual might begin with a prayer or a poem, a sacred act of anointing, or a meditation. It might include lighting a candle or burning incense.

When Lillian began thinking about a ritual to start her vigil, she liked the idea of incorporating symbolic acts that spoke of the give and take in life. She was very conscious of how much she had taken, in a positive sense, from friends and colleagues; how much she had accepted, absorbed, or learned. She had, in turn, tried to give to others in whatever ways she could. She had come to appreciate how this mutual exchange was at the heart of relationships. She combined these thoughts with her large collection of sea glass to come up with a unique ritual to start her vigil.

Lillian had collected sea glass during many summers spent wandering the beaches of Cape Cod. She loved the smooth, frosted appearance of these bits of broken bottles, jars, ship windows, and tableware that the ocean had tumbled and dragged around for thirty years or more until they were turned into little glass jewels.

At some point, while trying to figure out what to do with all of the sea glass, Lillian had started to string pieces together in long strands of various shades of green, blue, brown, and white with the very occasional pink, black, or a rare orange. At the end of the strand, on small rectangular pieces of heavy card stock, she would handwrite in beautiful script little fragments from her favorite poems. Because they were only bits of poems—like the bits of glass—they were enigmatic or provocative. Her family referred to them as "Lillian's fortunes," because the words reminded the family of the little strips of sayings in Chinese fortune cookies. The strands were hung in windows around the house to catch the light—there were dozens of them.

In the early night of the first day of her vigil, Lillian's close family and friends gathered to officially acknowledge the start of the vigil. One of her daughters read the vigil plan Lillian had created with the help of the doula and the family. Then they stood silently for a while. Candles flickered in the windows to create a soft, dancing light in the room.

Across a table at the foot of the bed, the family had draped many of Lillian's strands of sea glass. One by one, in no particular order, the people present would say something from their heart. Then they would take one of the strands of sea glass to hang in their own home as a way of remembering Lillian. The strands that were left at the end of the ritual were hung in the windows of Lillian's bedroom.

As is true of any ritual, ceremonial acts carry multiple meanings. For Lillian, another way of looking at the sea glass was to see in them the truth that the forces of life, well beyond our control, shape and mold who we are—softening our sharp edges over time, bringing out our inner beauty and wisdom. Life is the ocean that buffets and transforms us. Lillian knew that her death would be one of those buffeting experiences for the people who loved her. She accepted that without feeling sad about it, because she knew it was just one more way life would soften them and turn them into jewels.

Rituals can also play a part throughout the vigil. Some people start each day of the vigil with a ritual to mark that transition; others do so at the end of the day. These rituals may be as simple as lighting incense or a candle; saying a prayer; reading a poem; blessing the person dying and perhaps anointing them with water, oil, or wine; playing a particular piece of music; or doing a visualization. A ritual might be gathering everyone around the bed to speak from his or her heart, sing a song together, or chant.

Rituals play such important roles because they are designed by the dying person and the family. They reflect the personalities involved and embody a deep understanding about dying and the meaning of the dying person's life. They become way stations along the journey through the dying process, giving those present an opportunity to pause in the midst of focusing on care and thinking about loss to focus instead on the momentous nature of what is happening in that bed.

Ideas for rituals or parts of rituals may come from a person's religious tradition or their cultural background or from other traditions around the world. They can also be invented, using events, hobbies, travel experiences, or fragments of song as a starting point—there is no limit to the sources of ritual. As with guided imagery, the most powerful rituals are the ones that speak the most clearly about ideas or values held by the dying person and the family.

As the adult children in one family discussed a ritual that they could use to mark each day of the vigil, they came upon an idea based on something their mother Rose had done as a ritual in their early lives. When each of her five children had their first haircut, Rose would take a lock of hair, put it in an envelope with their name on it, and place it in a jewelry box that held other small symbols of their early life: a tooth, an award from school, a keychain they'd made at camp. So the children decided to start each new day of the vigil by cutting a lock of their hair and putting it in a small box to be buried with their mother.

While cutting locks of hair was a way to mirror in the present a ritual Rose had done in the past, it carried other meanings for them. The act of cutting represented how each day death was cutting their mother a little more out of their lives. On the other hand, burying those locks of hair with Rose symbolized that the connection could never be totally severed.

During the vigil, the story of what Rose's children were doing with their hair inspired other people to bring small symbolic gifts to be buried with her. For example, one friend brought a copy of a stained and tattered recipe that Rose had given her, with a message written on it about how delicious the recipe was and thanking Rose for the success the friend had each time she made it for company. A grandchild brought a little stuffed animal that Rose had thought was very cute; another grandchild brought a picture she had drawn of a path leading to heaven so that Rose would know what to look for and how to find it. These gifts were later mentioned at Rose's funeral.

Even planning a ritual can evoke deep feelings and may inspire a new understanding about the dying person or the meaning of this death in the lives of those left behind. Rituals should not only mark a transition from one reality to another but also bring comfort and help make the grief that follows a death easier to bear.

During the planning of a ritual, the doula will ask who should lead the ritual, who will be involved, and what objects, music, or words need to be gathered. Rituals should have a beginning, an ending, and a purpose people can articulate. Otherwise, there are no rules. Sometimes a vigil has multiple rituals: one to start it, another to start or end each day, one for right after the last breath, and another to begin the grieving process.

The ritual right after a person dies carries particular significance. After all, it marks the transition from a life to a death, the end of the journey through illness, the end of the vigil. Death is the moment the person and the family may have been dreading, but it also represents the end of a dying person's suffering.

When Barry took his last breath, his wife, two grown children, three grandchildren, and a couple of friends were at the bedside along with a doula. The shock of his last gasping inhalation, followed by an outbreath like blowing out a candle, stunned everyone into silence. They stood still and quiet, waiting to see if he would breathe again. But the waiting just continued and the silence grew deeper.

Without speaking, people reached out to hold hands. Perhaps it was that break in the stillness, but one of the grandchildren started to cry; it was like a crack spreading in a moan across a frozen lake. The parent of the child broke the ring of hands to embrace her daughter in a comforting hug.

"Grandpa will always be here with you," the mother of the child said, patting her daughter's chest at the heart. "Remember how he let you walk across his back when you were really little and jiggled to make you fall?"

"Yes," the girl said with a serious, sad expression still on her face. "He used to say that I tickled him like a butterfly. He said the same thing every time. Then we would both laugh."

With the silence broken, the doula announced that they should start the ritual Barry and his family had created for this moment. But because of the exchange that had just occurred between Barry's daughter and granddaughter, the doula suggested they add to the beginning of the ritual by giving each person a chance to say one thing they loved about Barry.

One of the other grandchildren then spoke. "I loved how Grandpa seemed to always smell of fresh baked bread and sweet pastry when he came home from working at the bakery." One of the adult children added, "Yes, like he was made from good, wholesome ingredients . . . you're so right." People mentioned how giving he was; how he never seemed to get angry at anyone;

how he loved a bargain in the supermarket and would buy ten of something he didn't even need because he was "saving money."

Then the doula asked Barry's wife and children to read the prayer "We Remember Them" together. The prayer by Sylvan Kamens and Rabbi Jack Riemer was originally written for the Reform Jewish liturgy, but it is also used by Unitarians, which was the church Barry had attended. It is a beautiful prayer that ties remembrance to the seasons in a very poetic way. It begins:

> At the rising of the sun and in its going down;
>> We remember them.
> At the blowing of the wind and in the chill of winter;
>> We remember them.
> At the opening of the buds and in the rebirth of spring;
>> We remember them.

The next part of the ritual was to wash Barry's body. His wife, Elizabeth, did this with the assistance of the doula, while everyone else went to the living room or the kitchen. In the living room, people looked through old photograph albums and told stories about Barry. His son sat at the piano and played whatever quiet music came to mind.

For the ritual of washing Barry's body, the doula had filled a bowl with warm water combined with a tablespoon of a premade mixture of finely ground oatmeal, baking soda, salt, and a drop of almond oil. These ingredients might be used to make bath oil, but they were also reminiscent of the ingredients that Barry used when baking bread or cookies. And almond was one of Barry's favorite flavors—he made wonderful almond croissants at the bakery. Elizabeth pulled out the clothes she wanted to dress him in after they were done washing him.

At the foot of the bed, the doula and Elizabeth set up a table, covered with one of Barry's washed aprons from the bakery. They placed the bowl of scented, floured water on the table, along with the watch Elizabeth had given him for their fiftieth wedding anniversary and a family picture taken at the party for that same anniversary. They put on a CD of Andrea Bocelli singing love songs, because Barry loved Bocelli. At the side of the bed on a night table, they lit a candle. Then they began removing the bedsheets and Barry's pajamas.

Elizabeth covered his genitals with a towel to preserve his dignity with the doula. Then the two of them silently dipped washcloths in the water and gently washed his body. They worked their way up his body from his feet. When it came to washing his genitals and rear end, Elizabeth did this by herself as the doula turned away. When they were done, they dressed him in the shirt and pants Elizabeth had chosen.

Then they called the family back into the room. So that everyone could feel that they had a part in the ritual cleansing of Barry's body, each person took a turn dipping a washcloth in the water and dabbing it on his face or hands and offering up a personal blessing.

His son touched both his hands with the washcloth and said, "I bless your hands that worked so hard all your life to support us and do for us." One daughter touched the washcloth to his lips and said, "I bless your lips that only uttered loving, kind words." His other daughter touched his eyelids and said, "I bless your eyes, which always seemed to smile with delight when your grandchildren were around." Elizabeth touched his forehead and said, "I bless your mind, which I always trusted to guide me when I was upset and didn't know what to do." And so on.

After putting away the bathwater and washcloths, the doula invited everyone to get a chair and sit around the bed so that they could keep looking over at Barry whenever they wanted to. They told stories about him and talked about the magic of the vigil time together. Hours went by. Only when the family started to get subdued again did the doula ask if it was time to call the funeral home to come and get him. The family all turned to Elizabeth to see how she felt. She nodded okay and cried softly. The doula went to make the call.

CHAPTER 11

The Vigil

It's inevitable. Terminal illness leads inexorably to the point at which the dying person's body can no longer hold back death. The twists and turns in the road along the way may vary from person to person, from one illness to another, but when the end is in sight, the signs and symptoms are quite similar.

The dying person can no longer eat, barely takes sips of fluid, may only mouth a word or two, and can hardly move a hand or leg. Their blood pressure drops dramatically from what was normal for them, and there is a corresponding increase in the pulse rate, which is more irregular in strength and rhythm. Dramatic changes occur in breathing, slowing or speeding up—sometimes both—with pauses between that can go on for up to a minute.

All the autonomic systems of the body go haywire. The person may spike a fever for no apparent reason; the color of their skin changes. Their eyes may stay partly open without blinking, but it's also clear that they aren't seeing.

It is the entire constellation of these signs and symptoms that indicate a person has entered the last days or hours of life. This period of time is referred to as "active dying," a phrase that implies the body is now shutting down and has no chance of coming back. Generally, a nurse or a doctor will decide when a person starts to die actively. But there is no exact science to making that determination—it is always a judgment call based on experience. The vigil should begin as soon as a person has entered this stage.

The first sign that George was getting close to the time for a vigil was when he repeatedly refused food over a period of several days. His wife, Helen, offered him the foods he loved the most, but George kept saying he didn't want any. He didn't seem to have any difficulty swallowing. He said the food didn't have any taste to him, and he just didn't feel like eating.

Often families struggle a great deal when their loved one refuses to eat. Most people equate food with life. They feel that as long as the person is eating, they will stay alive. Even more devastating is the belief that if they stop offering food, they are starving the person to death.

Helen had been well prepared by the nurse, so she understood that pushing food on George was wrong. She knew that he could aspirate and literally choke to death if he didn't swallow properly. She also knew that while his refusal to eat appeared to be a conscious or willful choice on his part—because he spoke about it with words like, "I just don't feel like eating"—it was really an indication that his body could no longer digest the food properly.

Death is a natural process of the body breaking down. As the internal systems that automatically manage the body's functions shut down, other built-in mechanisms take over to aid in the process of dying. The fact that food loses its taste and appeal is one of the mechanisms that aids the body as the digestive functions shut down. In a sense, the body is designed to die. Since this is a natural process, family can help a dying person most when they surrender to the process.

One afternoon, after perhaps five days of George not eating, Helen went in to check on him. He had continued to drink, and she was bringing him a cup of watered-down mango juice with a straw. He was still sleeping, as he had been all morning, which was happening more in the last several days. While she stood and watched him, she noticed that he stopped breathing for about five seconds. That night, he was very restless in bed and kept trying to change position. No matter what Helen did to make him more comfortable, it didn't last for more than fifteen or twenty minutes.

The nurse from hospice came the following day and gave him a new medication to help with his restlessness. His vital signs were still in the normal range for him. Helen saw pauses in his breath several times, now for up to ten seconds.

Two days later, Helen couldn't rouse George. He did open his eyes slightly when she and a home health aide washed and changed him, but his eyes didn't stay open for more than a few seconds, and he wasn't able to speak. Helen thought that he did respond yes to a question with a slight nod, he just didn't have the energy to respond more fully.

Helen called the nurse to let her know what was happening. The nurse came that afternoon and saw that his vital signs were markedly different. His blood pressure was much lower than it had been, and his pulse was well above normal. He was breathing through an open mouth somewhat rapidly, and it was labored. The nurse told Helen that it was time to call the doulas to start the vigil.

Doula work with the dying is different from that at a birth. A woman's active labor period is generally about eight to twelve hours and is unlikely to go on for more than eighteen hours. One birth doula can work with a woman through her entire labor.

The active dying process takes, on average, two to four days but can go on for ten days. One death doula can't possibly serve throughout the entire labor of dying if a doula is going to be there for the majority of the process. End-of-life doulas typically work in groups. If each doula takes a twelve-hour shift, it can take four or more doulas to cover a vigil around the clock for multiple days, which is what the doulas hope to do. If doulas can work only in four- to six-hour shifts, then the group must be larger.

One of the longer vigils I led went on for eight and a half days. In total, it lasted for 206 hours. Because the vigil was a service that hospice provided, the doulas did shifts that averaged only four hours. In the end, the vigil took fifty-one shifts and involved twenty-three different doulas—some of whom did as many as four shifts.

The doula who took the first shift with George and Helen arrived in the middle of the afternoon. She focused on setting up the environment according to the vigil plan. She made sure that all the medical supplies and medications were either out of the room or out of sight in prearranged places that were easy to access. With the help of a couple of other people, the bed was pulled away from the wall so that more people could sit around the bed and get close to George.

The bed had been against the wall because in the week just before the vigil, George had been restless and would try to get out of the bed on his own during the night. But he couldn't take more than a step or two before his legs would give out, and the family didn't want him to fall and get hurt. Helen slept on the open side of the bed, so she would wake up if he tried to get out. Then she could convince him to stay in bed or at least help him safely get to the bathroom. Now that he was in a coma-like state, he wasn't trying to get up.

The doula made sure that the music George wanted was next to the CD player and put on his favorite Gregorian chant album, *Chant Music for the Soul,* by the Cistercian Monks of Stift Heiligenkreuz. There were other Gregorian chant albums, as well as CDs with nature sounds.

The doula also asked Helen for a small rug that she placed at the entrance to the bedroom and posted a sign at the doorway right above the rug that read: "Before Entering, Please Remove Your Shoes and Offer a Prayer of Thanks." Helen placed a pair of George's shoes right below the sign on the rug, acknowledging that George had left the world behind, the world where he needed shoes. He had entered the room for the rest of his life.

A couple of months earlier, George had planned a ceremony to officially begin the vigil. It was to take place as soon after the start of the vigil as possible, allowing for people to arrive—including the doula he had worked with to plan the vigil. Since the first shift started in the afternoon, the ritual was to take place around 8:00 in the evening. Everyone gathered around George and Helen's bed. Those present included Helen, their son and daughter, George's brother and sister-in-law, a nephew and his wife, along with several friends. They had all removed their shoes at the entrance of the room, placing them on the mat alongside George's shoes.

Helen put on *Chant Music for the Soul* again, so it would play quietly in the background. The doula directed everyone to hold hands and close their eyes. She asked them to hold in their mind the image of George's face wearing his incredibly boyish smile. Then the doula read a letter George had written for the occasion.

In it, he expressed his love for his family and friends. He asked that everyone, starting at this moment, focus on all the wonderful memories of their times together—the fun they'd had, the laughs, the quiet moments of appreciation, walks in the woods, discoveries of new places, sharing children, deep conversations on profound questions. He wanted them to speak to each other and to him of these things throughout the vigil.

When the doula finished the letter, she asked everyone to open their eyes and focus on George's face as each one offered up a wish for how he and Helen would experience these last days. After everyone had spoken, the doula read them the plan that she and George had worked out for the vigil. It noted the music and readings he wanted, the visualization, and described how he wanted to be touched and held.

After reading the plan, the doula asked Helen to light a tall, purple candle, similar to a sanctuary candle, that was supposed to burn for at least seven days. They intended to extinguish the candle as part of the ritual after he died. Lighting the candle ended the ritual. Helen made tea and everyone went into the living room to share time together while the doula sat at George's bedside.

As they talked about the ritual and shared how touched they were by it, George's brother said that he would like to stay with George for as much time as possible. Other people said they would like to do the same. A spontaneous discussion ensued that led to a plan. With Helen's approval, the family and friends present decided to sit shifts with the doulas. One of them would always be at the bedside day and night, even if they were just sleeping on the floor. In this way, they would be sure that George wouldn't die without a family member or friend present, even if his death came suddenly—which can happen sometimes. This was their way of demonstrating their devotion to George and returning the love he had so freely offered each of them.

Many times, as a vigil advances, people begin to learn how profound sitting vigil can be. Without ever consciously discussing it, people get inspired to enter into a dynamic, sacred dance of physical care, touch, speaking from the heart, and following the model the doulas establish. Death becomes less frightening. Instead, it becomes an honored rite of passage.

People who participate in a vigil with doulas can never again experience death in a disconnected and anxious way. Future deaths, even their own—when the time comes—will be filled with tenderness, peace, and a deep appreciation for the momentous nature of this passage.

The primary aim of the vigil is to hold the space for the kind of dying experience the dying person and the family want. This is why the planning work in the months or weeks before the vigil is so important. It gives the dying person and others the opportunity to think and feel their way into what would make the last days meaningful.

As with so many aspects of this work, the nature of a plan and its details depend on the personality and ideas of the person dying and the family. For that reason, each plan is unique. Some are highly detailed and programmatic; others speak more to the overall spirit of the vigil and specify few details. Some plans are focused on the wishes of the person dying and what will make them most comfortable; others deal more with wishes of the family and what will help them get through the experience of the last days.

Plans aren't static documents. Every vigil will include things that were never discussed or built into the plan, things that need to be modified in the plan or dropped altogether. The doulas stay in touch with what is happening around them by observing everything and by staying connected to the intuitive part of their minds. This is what it means to offer engaged presence when you are sitting vigil.

Presence isn't an easy concept to talk about. It means opening to what is happening in the moment. The doula focuses the beam of attention on any activity they are doing with the dying person or the family. At the same time, they stretch their awareness wider to capture what is happening beyond the immediate focus. It is holding this split-screen-like focus, as much as possible, that allows the doula to slip into the mind-state of presence.

When a person is fully present in this way, they bring all of themselves, and especially their intuitive instincts, into the moment. Being fully present, a doula will feel an inner still-ness and openness. When you receive information intuitively, it comes with a sense of "aha-ness"; there aren't doubts or judg-ments. Sometimes you respond to a situation very quickly with-out thinking; at other times the knowing arrives over time until it's fully clear. And that knowing can come in the form of a word or phrase or as a feeling.

One of the most powerful experiences I have had with presence happened during a vigil for a woman I had met briefly only a couple of times. Her daughter-in-law was the primary caregiver. I came to do a shift in the late afternoon. The dying woman's only grandchildren, who also lived in the house, hadn't yet come home from school. The woman's son was a high-level investment banker who worked long hours and wouldn't be home until later in the evening. The daughter-in-law was very fearful of having her mother-in-law die while she was there alone with her.

After quickly checking in on the dying woman to make sure she wasn't imminent, I went downstairs to the kitchen to talk to the daughter-in-law. She gave me an update on what had been happening over the last day. Then I asked her to come upstairs with me to spend some more time talking as we stayed at the bedside.

I checked on the number of breaths per minute and watched for signs of change in the breathing pattern. Her breath came slow and even but very shallow, like a whisper. Only her upper chest seemed to rise and fall. I also felt the pulse in her wrist, which was irregular, changing from firm to faint, feeling sometimes broken, a more rapid beat for several seconds and then slower or not present. These patterns were about the same as I had observed the day before.

At my prompting, the daughter-in-law told me stories about the woman and how having her live with the family had affected the household. As we were talking, I heard the woman's breathing change. When I looked over, I saw that it was more shallow than just minutes ago, each breath beginning with a quick gasp of air. Her hands were cold and her fingernail beds were turning blue to purple. These signs might indicate hours to live, but my intuitive sense was that she had only minutes.

All of these changes were abrupt and unexpected. But sometimes this happens, as if the person suddenly decided to die. I told her I was going to caress her forehead. I felt warmth emanating from the top of her head as my hand passed over it. I closed my eyes for a moment and my mind was filled with the vision of a column of white light. I told her that I could see where she was and that she should go toward the light as soon as she felt ready.

The daughter-in-law came over to stand by my side. I reassured the dying woman that she was doing exactly what she needed to. "I can feel that you're moving toward the light now,"

I said. "Just keep doing what feels good to you." Then I added, "Your son and daughter-in-law are in a good place with each other, and they're raising two fine children. You have given them everything they need for their lives to continue well. Don't be concerned for them." Her breath became even more faint; the gasping had stopped. I could feel something ease in her body.

"It's okay, Mom," said her daughter-in-law, as she placed her hand on top of her mother-in-law's hand. "Jamie and the kids will miss you, but they will always think of you with love." I could feel that she was just moments away.

A stillness that seemed to hum with energy filled the room. I closed my eyes again and saw nothing but a white, vibrant energy. "I can see that you have already entered the light," I said, my eyes open again and focused on her face. "Just let it bring you to where you need to go." With that she took in one slightly deeper breath, exhaled more deeply as well, and stopped breathing. Her face relaxed and oddly seemed more alive than before.

Although we waited several minutes to watch for more breath, we knew she had died. Then the room became brighter. Perhaps it was the sun coming out from behind a cloud and shining in through the window. Or perhaps it was the woman's spirit filling the room.

The daughter-in-law looked over at me, but neither of us spoke, not wanting to break the stillness. Finally, she said, "That was amazing. As you know, I have been terrified at the thought of being with her at the end. But it was so peaceful, and I could feel her presence in the room after she died. I will never forget these last few minutes. They are a blessing. Jamie will be so glad when I tell him how it went. I'm going to call him right now."

Intuitive moments aren't always as dramatic as this. But over the years I have experienced many similar, wonderful moments. All the doulas I have worked with have these experiences too, as they stay highly focused and intently present in their work.

Each vigil establishes its own rhythm, given the plan the dying person and the family worked out, the mood of the vigil as it develops, the interactions of the doulas with the family, and the changing nature of the circumstances. The plan establishes what I think of as the outer shape of the vigil: the music, readings, touch, guided visualization, continued legacy work, and rituals.

The inner experience of the vigil is the more unstructured, organic exchange that occurs between all the participants. This can never be planned; it just unfolds. Yet this is the heart of the vigil, the space in which the most profound gifts happen.

As the vigil for George progressed, a deep sense of sacredness grew from the quiet, intimate atmosphere that had been established by the beginning ritual. It was what George had hoped for, even though he recognized that it couldn't be planned for directly. The decision by family and friends to hold vigil around the clock alongside the doulas also contributed to the sacred feeling in the room.

I have often felt the cumulative effect of presence, as each person brings their own heart to the bedside and to one another. If something happens that feels spontaneous, it isn't just what that particular doula or family member did just then, rather it is the whole accumulation of the moment-to-moment offerings of presence from all the people involved that led to it.

Although I had spent some time with George and his family, through the first two days of his vigil, my first formal shift started at midnight on the second day. I was to be there until six o'clock the following morning. As soon as I entered George's room, I could feel the sacred intimacy held in the space. Most everyone was either resting or asleep, except for George's brother, Dean, who was sitting at the bedside when I arrived.

I spent the first fifteen minutes getting an update from the doula who was there before me. She told me that George's condition hadn't really changed during her shift—so it was more or less the same as the day before.

The hand-off update between one doula and the next helps the replacement doula understand what has happened over the previous shift and alerts the new doula to any events or behaviors that he or she should know about. The departing doula will also let the next shift doula know if they used visualization, touch, music, or reading.

After the previous doula and I had finished the hand-off report, I went in to sit at the bedside with George's brother. Then I asked him to give me a sense of how things were going from his perspective.

"I never would have imagined that sitting with my brother as he was dying could feel so holy," he said. "That feeling started with the beginning ritual. I think all of us enter this room as if it's a temple and take care of George or just sit beside him as if those actions are prayers we offer to him."

I was struck by how deep and pervasive the mood of sacredness was in this vigil. I think it was a testimony to the family. They had embraced the doula approach so quickly and completely. Although they had never experienced a dying process like this one, they joined with the doulas fully.

I asked Dean to tell me about George. He said that George was a very good, loving man, who had also been a great brother. He told me stories about George lending people money when they needed it, without them ever asking. And how he never asked for it back, trusting that they would pay him in their own time. Dean also spoke about George's dedication to his church. He went to services every Sunday without fail and took a very active role in several committees.

After talking with me for a while, Dean said that he needed to rest a bit and went to the recliner in a corner of the room. He told me that according to the schedule the family had worked out, Helen was due to replace him after several hours.

Helen came into the room earlier than expected. She stood at the foot of the bed, looking at George. "I couldn't really sleep," she said. "But at least I had a chance to lie down and rest. I think I have been revved up from the beginning of the vigil, and the steady rain tonight didn't let me fall asleep." The rain was insistent and noisy on the roof. It sounded like a shuffling, marching parade of feet that kept going on and on.

Helen came to sit next to me and asked how George was doing. I told her that he hadn't really changed. Before she came in, I had taken careful note of his breathing, which was still in the normal range, averaging twelve breaths per minute. He had very short periods of apnea—only five to six seconds—every so often. There wasn't a lot of light in the room, because there was only one table lamp that cast a cream-colored light across the bed and into the room, so I couldn't examine George's color well. But it still seemed more normal than not. And his pulse was only slightly elevated.

One of the things I always do when I'm sitting vigil is to regularly note the frequency and pattern of breathing and check the pulse. These two signs are good indictors of what is happening and reflect further breakdown in the body. Doulas note the smallest changes to the signs and symptoms of dying so that they can explain them to the family and prepare them for what is coming.

These regular assessments of the dying person's condition are part of the rhythm of vigil service. When observed carefully, the signs and symptoms help a doula know when a person's death is imminent. At that point, they will call family into the room for the last breaths.

After Helen had settled in her chair, we both became quiet, just watching the rise and fall of George's chest as he breathed. The silence between us seemed to expand, filling the room, and it deepened as the sound of the rain encouraged a feeling of reverie. Without saying anything, I gently put my hand on top of Helen's, knowing that it would be okay because touch was already a part of how I had comforted her in the past. With her other hand, she squeezed my hand and held it firmly.

We sat in the quiet for a while longer, then Helen turned to me and said, "There's something I've been meaning to talk to you about. I know you may not have an answer you feel comfortable sharing, but I thought with all your experience helping other people through this, that you might have a better idea than most people. What do you think happens after we die?"

I could feel that her question wasn't idle curiosity, nor was it desperate. It felt like it came from a deep place of searching for a belief she could hold on to. "What prompted that question at this moment?" I asked her, trying to go deeper into what she needed to talk about.

"Well, it is something I've wondered about from time to time over the course of my life. But ever since George was diagnosed, it has come up for me quite a bit. As I was lying in bed before, my mind went to that question, and I realized that it didn't really matter to me what the afterlife might be like. Of course, I hope for his sake that he goes to the heaven his Catholic faith taught him about. But when I try to think about George after he dies, what I would like to be reassured about is that he will be okay. I want to know that he won't just disappear completely. How could it be that all he felt, thought, and did over eighty or so years simply vanishes? Does that question make sense?"

"Of course it makes sense. Tell me what you think it would mean for George to be okay after death."

"That he won't suffer anymore. This illness has been so unkind to him, taking away his energy, his independence, his ability to function as a husband and a father, and of course the wasting of his body . . . and the pain. He never complained, mind you. But I just don't want to see him suffer anymore."

"I know you realize that I can't really answer your question about what happens after death, or for that matter tell you definitively that George will be okay. No one can. I know that for some people, prayer helps with this kind of concern. Would that help you?"

"I've never felt as connected to my religion as George does. I was raised as a Christian, not Catholic, and my family was very loose about their beliefs. Of course I have prayed at times, but I doubt my prayers are heard. When I have prayed, it isn't so much about being answered; it's more about me voicing my deepest longings and sometimes my scariest thoughts."

"Have you felt better after praying in that way?"

"I guess in some way."

"There is something I sometimes say to people who are dying that is like a prayer but not religious. It involves only three phrases that can be repeated or expanded as a person sees fit. I can say it now for George, and, if it feels good to you, it is something that you can say for him after he dies whenever your concern about his being okay comes up in your mind. Would you like me to do that?"

"Yes, please."

As I continued to hold Helen's hand, I gently put my other hand on George's forehead and started to speak softly. "May you be filled with light. May you be free of all suffering. And may you be at peace."

I asked Helen to repeat those three phrases with me. Helen placed her other hand on George's leg, so we were both connected to him physically. Then we said those three phrases together.

"When I say this prayer internally or out loud, I usually do it three times," I said. "The first time I say it as we just did. Then I go back to the first phrase and expand it in a way that feels right at the moment and reflects what I know about the person. Something like this: George, may you be filled with light; the light that has been sent to you over the years from all the people you love and those who love you. The light that comes from your deep faith in God; the light at the very core of your being that you share with all beings; the light that you may see waiting for you as you get closer to that which separates this world from the next.

"May you be free of all suffering; the suffering that your illness has brought to your body; the suffering of anticipating a time that your family will be without you; the suffering of missed opportunities in the past or memories of times that you weren't able to live up to your highest expectations for yourself.

"And may you be at peace; the peace that comes to all of us from accepting that we have done the best we could in our lives; the peace of knowing that you were loved and have freely given your love to others; the peace of letting go of the body that sustained you but must be left behind; the peace of moving into the fullness of your communion with the God you know.

"I like to speak this middle section of the prayer spontaneously, so it connects to my feeling and intuition of the moment.

"Then, after these expanded phrases, I usually finish with the simple version of the prayer again: May you be filled with light; may you be free of all suffering; and may you be at peace.

"You can say this prayer as often as you like, and I think it has great power for the person you say it to as well as for yourself. It doesn't replace any other prayers that you feel would be appropriate, but you can add it to the prayers you say. In a way, I think it expresses your wish that George will be okay—now and after he dies."

Helen thanked me and told me that she felt much better. During the next several hours, I could see Helen mouthing the prayer to herself a few times. At some point, George spiked a fever, which is a very natural part of the dying process. We applied a cool compress and pulled back the blanket from his upper chest so that his body might cool down.

Perhaps a couple of hours after Helen had come into the room, Dean woke up. Seeing Helen there, he checked in briefly, then went off to get some more sleep in his bed. At one point, I gave Helen about thirty minutes alone with George so that she wouldn't feel self-conscious talking to him out loud and saying what she needed to. We had talked in the past about the importance of continuing to express love and to offer forgiveness for the inevitable hurt we cause even to the people we love in close relationship.

I spent those thirty minutes in the kitchen with George's daughter, who wandered in from a fitful sleep. I offered to make her some tea, which she accepted, and then we talked for a little bit about how her father was doing before she decided to try to get some more rest.

The doula's job is to see or intuit what can be done here and now that will be the most supportive to the dying person or the family. Do they need a cup of tea, a reminder to have something to eat, a couple hours of rest, an arm around their shoulder to let them know you feel with them, a quiet acceptance of what they need to say without judging them for something that might be harsh, painful, confused, or just different from what you might do or say in a similar moment?

For the person dying, the doula will consider the plan that has been developed and what in that plan makes sense in that moment. The doula will decide if it is time to play the Frank Sinatra CD, read from the book of Mary Oliver poems, offer a guided visualization, or simply hold the person's hand or caress their head. Depending on circumstances, the doula will consult with a family member about what feels right to them or make a suggestion based on the moment.

Ultimately, of course, there is no one right thing. Each doula has their own sense of what is needed in the moment, based on their experience, who they are as a person, and what they know about the people involved. But, by trying to stay true to the spirit of the plan and the feeling of the moment, a doula's intuition will mostly be right.

When I talk to family during and after a vigil to find out what went well and what didn't, I almost always hear that the doulas seemed to have this amazing capacity to do exactly the right thing at the right time. I could cite so many examples of this from the hundreds of vigils I have been part of. In the early morning hours of my shift, we experienced one of those moments.

The rain had let up to become a soft pattering on the roof, but the wind had picked up. There was a wooden chime outside the bedroom window somewhere that played a haphazard tune, sounding like an African thumb piano. George's daughter Cynthia came wandering into the room in her pajamas, rubbing her eyes. "Something woke me, maybe the wind, so I thought I would check on Dad," she said. "How is he doing?"

"There really hasn't been any change," I told her. "Your mom and I have just been quietly talking, holding his hand, and caressing his head."

"Has he responded in any way or seemed in pain?"

"No, he seems peaceful and very deep inside."

"I think I'll stay for a while," she said as she pulled up a chair to the opposite side of the bed from where Helen and I were sitting.

We sat silently together for a while, just listening to George's breathing, the light rain, and the crazy tune of the wooden chime—sometimes loud, at other moments faint but present. As the silence grew, it felt oddly comforting and seemed to help me feel closer to Cynthia, whom I hadn't talked with as much as Helen and some of the other family.

Finally, I asked, "What are you thinking about right now?"

"I was just remembering how Dad and I would play hide-and-seek when I was a kid. I would get so excited when he would loudly clomp around as he got close, saying 'fee-fi-fo-fum, I smell the blood of a tasty, sweet little girl named Cynthi-yum.' I could hardly contain a squeal of fear and delight. Then he would grab me up and twirl me around as he tickled my sides and kissed my cheeks.

"I would look into his eyes that were such a beautiful blue and feel so warm and safe. I don't think I have ever felt as safe as when I was in his arms. I wish I could look into his beautiful eyes again and see one more time that wonderful twinkle when he scooped me up."

George hadn't responded in any way for the past four or five days. He hadn't opened his eyes, moved his arms or legs, or even tried to speak. This is often hard for the family, because they want so much to know that their dying loved one realizes they are there with them and doing their best to comfort them.

Doulas often tell people to keep talking to their loved one—to tell the person that they love them, to reassure them that they will be okay, and to let go when the time is right for them to do so. But without getting a response, it's hard to hold on to the belief that saying things makes a difference.

It occurred to me as I listened to Cynthia that she might feel comforted by lying next to her father. It wasn't something we had talked about doing, but I know that lying in bed and getting close with your whole body can bring a tremendous feeling of peace. Perhaps it would give Cynthia that same feeling of being safe that she had felt as a little girl in his arms.

"Why don't you lie in bed next to your dad and tell him the same story about hide-and-seek."

Cynthia lay on her side next to her dad, propped up on her elbow, and leaned over his face to speak the story closer to his ear. Even though his face was sunken and narrowed by his illness, I could see the resemblance in her mouth and nose. "I think I just saw his eyelids flutter, as if he was trying to open them," she said.

"This may be a good moment to tell him again how much you love him," I said.

She put her hand on the side of his face as she got even closer. "I love you so much, Dad. You're the best man I know, maybe even better than Paul [her husband]."

At that moment, George's eyes opened and he seemed to look directly at his daughter, recognizing her. Then he mouthed the words, "I love you, too." His eyes closed again. Cynthia started crying, as did Helen and I.

"Did you see that?" Cynthia said. "He does know we're here."

That was the last time George opened his eyes more than a slit or tried to speak. To all of us, it felt like his last gift. He didn't die until two days later, but this unexpected moment felt filled with love, and I knew that Cynthia would cherish it for the rest of her life. Whenever she thinks about her dad, that memory will rise up in her and make her feel loved and safe.

Throughout the rest of the vigil for George, the family and the doulas sat in shifts together, continuing to use George's guided visualization of lying on a moss-covered forest floor by the side of a stream, hearing the water splash around rocks as he stared up through the treetops to a perfect blue sky without even a hint of clouds. There was a CD called *Forest Stream* that we would play at times during the visualization. There are a great many recordings available that have nature sounds or gentle instrumental music that make a wonderful background for visualizations.

The doulas and the family took turns reading to George, and everyone continued to touch and hold him. The story of Cynthia climbing in bed with him and what happened spread among the family. Helen and George's other daughter also spent time snuggled up with George for periods of time. One of the doulas showed Helen how she could climb in bed behind George to have him resting up against her chest. The secretions in his chest accumulated over the days of the vigil, and this position kept him more upright and helped ease the rattling sounds in his breathing.

As George got closer to dying, we stopped this kind of holding so as not to disturb him as much. There comes a point at which too much shifting and moving of a person may interfere with the process of letting go. When we get to that point in a vigil, touch should be light and very gentle. Stroking should be almost like water running over the skin. Reading, music, and visualization should continue, as it is soothing to the person dying and also helps the caregivers.

Through the five days of his vigil, George slowly declined and seemed to move deeper inside and further away from those around him. His breathing became more and more shallow, and there were longer periods of apnea. On the last day, he was breathing only five to six times a minute with pauses after every few exhalations that lasted around thirty seconds each time. The color drained out of his face, so he looked pasty. His pulse became more irregular and disappeared at times, true signs that death was getting closer.

George died almost exactly five days after the vigil had begun. Since the doula who was present for the death had recognized that George's death was imminent, everyone who needed to be there for the last breaths was there. Helen, her daughters, Dean and his wife—they were all around the bedside, holding each other, continuing to talk to George, expressing love and reassuring him that they would take care of one another.

His last breath was just a puff of exhalation, but people somehow knew that it was the last breath. Although they waited a couple of minutes to be sure, they all knew he had died on that breath. There was some gentle crying. Cynthia leaned over and lay her upper body across George's chest, embracing him with both arms and saying, "I love you, Daddy." Helen rubbed her back in support. The doula went over and put her arm around Helen's shoulder.

After allowing some silent time for everyone to stay with their feelings, the doula told people that they could remain as long as they wanted at the bedside—to continue talking to George and touching or kissing him. She called the doula who had performed the ritual at the start of the vigil so that she could come back to lead the ritual created to mark his death. Then she called the hospice to ask for a nurse to come and pronounce George dead.

By the time the nurse had finished the pronouncement and disposed of the medications, the doula who was to lead the ceremony had arrived. She put a small table at the foot of the bed, along with the still-burning purple candle. On the table, she placed a handmade box with the decoupage image of the Virgin of Guadalupe, the rays of the sun emanating from all around her standing figure, the moon at her feet.

It was a favorite image of George's. He had selected this box to hold his ashes after his cremation. Although cremation isn't common for Catholics, that was what George had wanted. Also on the table were the two urns holding his mother's and father's ashes.

The doula started the ceremony by telling everyone that George had requested they mark his death with this ritual. For background sound, the doula pulled up a Sound Scapes recording, *Distant Trains Echoing in the Rain*, on a computer. George had told the doula that he loved hearing the distant sound of the freight train that went through town in the middle of the night. George thought the sound of the train was mournful but also inviting.

The doula had found this particular recording, which George said was exactly like the train sounds he heard when the train passed through town a couple of miles away. He wanted it played during the ceremony because he liked the symbolism of being carried away by the train.

To the echoing sound of the train, everyone was asked to write a last few words to George on slips of paper that were handed around. Each person took a turn placing their paper into the box with the image of the Virgin of Guadalupe. The messages would later be burned with George's body so that they would be part of the ashes that went into the box.

Then Helen opened the urns of George's parents. She took what looked like a makeup brush and dipped into one urn, announcing that this was the ash of George's mother that he had requested be placed in his right hand. She brushed it across his palm, leaving a residue of grey ash. Then she did the same from the urn with his father's ashes, brushing them across George's left palm.

The doula explained that George thought having the ashes of his parents in the palms of his hands would help him to see them on the other side. He also liked the idea of his ashes containing some of theirs, comingled, the way his body was a merging of their genes. After George's ashes were placed in the box, it was to be buried in a local Catholic cemetery with his parents' urns alongside it.

To end the ceremony, Dean read a prayer that George had selected:

God our Father,
Your power brings us to birth,
Your providence guides our lives,
and by Your command we return to dust.

Lord, those who die still live in Your presence,
their lives change but do not end.
I pray in hope for my family,
relatives and friends,
and for all the dead known to You alone.

In company with Christ,
Who died and now lives,
may they rejoice in Your kingdom,
where all our tears are wiped away.
Unite us together again in one family,
to sing Your praise forever and ever.

Amen.

Then Dean blew out the purple candle that had been burning since the start of the vigil. For several minutes, everyone stood just where they were, watching the smoke from the extinguished candle twist upward and dissipate slowly in the air. The train whistles echoed in the background.

As is usual, the doula who led the ceremony and the doula who had been there for George's last breaths stayed for hours after the ceremony. Emotional support for the family right after a person dies is part of the work doulas do. They will stay as long as the family needs them.

Doulas will often stand in for the family to watch over the funeral home staff that come to take the body, since the family may not want to watch this process. The doula can make sure the body is handled respectfully and bear witness to the departure, sometimes covering the body with a cloth or blanket that has special meaning to the family to make it easier to watch this leave-taking. Even after the body is gone, the doulas will continue to provide support, if the family asks them to stay.

When the doulas leave after death, that doesn't end their service to the family. They will go back three to six weeks later to reprocess the experience and to discuss the nature of grieving and what people need to do to heal well.

The days that follow a death are usually filled with activity around preparations for the viewing and then the funeral. Often, family or friends from out of town come to stay with those in mourning. During this in-between time, the doula who led the rituals and I called Helen a couple of times to provide a few minutes of support over the phone. I went to a viewing and the funeral, as did a number of the doulas from the vigil.

Often, the family feels that this time is surreal. They can't fully comprehend that their loved one has really died. This is why the reprocessing visits that begin a number of weeks after a death are so important. When the first of those visits occurred with Helen, her two daughters were there, along with Dean and his wife. The six doulas who attended that session and I were welcomed as if we were family—and in some magical way, because of the intimacy of the vigil time, we were.

CHAPTER 12

Reprocessing and Grief

When doulas return to visit family some weeks after a death, their primary goal is to help family understand the dying experience they have so recently lived through. They lead the family through an examination of the physical decline, the staggering challenges they faced in caring for their loved one, the roller coaster ride of emotions, and the indelible moments of love and insight.

There is perhaps no other common human experience with such intense highs and lows compressed into only a few days. Nor is there a human experience that can scar so deeply or offer such rich opportunity for self-discovery. Its impact can reverberate across the lives of survivors until they die. At the same time, it is terrain we must all traverse at some point.

This reprocessing work can occur in one visit, or it can span a series of visits. It generally starts with telling the story of the dying process—what people saw, heard, felt, said, and did—all the experiences they went through, from their perspective and that of their loved one who died. Story is at the heart of how we come to understand our experience, digest it, learn from it, and finally let go of the pieces that may hold us back from living our lives with purpose and joy. The trek through grief demands we tell the story over and over. We can't recover or heal without story. It gives structure and form to our experiences.

As the family tells their story and begins giving it shape, the doulas can help mold it from their position as outsiders who also became participants right alongside the family. The doulas share their emotions and insights, which can impact the way the family sees and understands their experience.

"Do you remember our first meeting?" Rose asked me. We were sitting in a brick-walled back room of an Italian restaurant in New York City. We had come together to talk about the vigil we had done for Rose's son Paul. Besides Rose and her husband, there were four doulas, including me, and the close friend who had taken care of Paul during the eight months of his battle against cancer. The waiter had just taken our lunch orders, so we now had the room all to ourselves.

"Yes, I do," I answered. "You were pacing up and down in the long, narrow living room of Paul's apartment." Paul's vigil was one of the earliest I had led. Rose had come from out of state to help care for her son in the last month or so of his illness.

"I remember that a young woman friend of Paul's was visiting then as well," I continued. "She hadn't seen him since she got pregnant and thought this would be the last time she and her husband could come. It was quite important to her because of how much she loved and respected Paul. She wanted Paul to hold his hands on her belly so that she could feel that her baby and Paul had connected. I was very touched by the tenderness of that act. It was the first indication to me of how special Paul was to his friends."

"I had forgotten that Astrid was there that time," Rose said. "Thank you for reminding me. What I remember best about that meeting was how anxious I was. I had only been here in the city for about two weeks. I wasn't sleeping, I couldn't sit down. He was doing so poorly then. He couldn't support his own weight any longer or speak above a whisper. All I kept thinking was I can't believe my son is dying. How am I ever going to get through it?"

"I think you said almost those exact words to me right after I introduced myself. What I heard beneath those words was a feeling that you wouldn't survive his death."

"But you calmed me down right away. Over the next week or so, I started to believe that I could make it. And more than that, I realized I could move past my fear to focus on caring for him. That was quite a gift."

"That wasn't my doing. I think that knowing the doulas would be there to assist and guide you was reassuring. It probably helped to loosen the knots of anxiety. But the transformation you experienced came from inside you. I saw it happening in our discussions about Paul's legacy and in the way you took on more and more of the caregiving; a gradual rediscovery of a strength that's just part of who you are."

The reprocessing went on for over three hours. We reviewed every important aspect of a vigil that had lasted for four days. Each day of that vigil, something came up that challenged Rose and helped her open more deeply to the experience. For example, on the second day, we discussed her saying it was okay for Paul to let go, which she said she couldn't do. But by that night, she had.

Perhaps her biggest breakthrough was deciding to wash Paul's body right after he died. We had talked about it a couple of times, but Rose couldn't decide how she felt about it. I had arrived for a shift that was due to start at midnight, only to discover that Paul had died ten minutes earlier. Right after I got there, Rose announced that she wanted to wash Paul's body. The doula whom I was supposed to replace, Rose, and I did this last act of caring for his body. It was the first time I had ever done this. We didn't talk. Each of us helped the others and did what needed to be done.

It all flowed so naturally together and felt incredibly spiritual, as if we were praying. His body seemed to glow in the dim candlelit bedroom. I remember looking over at Rose's face and seeing this beatific expression. I was not surprised when, at the reprocessing, Rose said she had felt euphoric as we washed Paul's body.

As the reprocessing with Rose came to an end, I needed to say something more to her. "Paul's vigil taught me a great many things. I came to see how we can hold pain and love in equal measure and look unflinchingly into the heart of death. That is where we can find what makes us most human and most holy. I also became convinced through our collective experience that the doula approach, which I had learned from birth doulas, was exactly the right approach at the end of life. That was your gift to me."

Reprocessing sessions also uncover the more traumatic moments of the dying process—the ones that can get imbedded in a person's mind, like shrapnel from a bomb. Trauma may result from things seen or heard, from words spoken or unsaid, from events that occurred or didn't. These moments may play over and over again in a person's mind, keeping them trapped in negative emotions.

Everyone who goes through the death of a loved one has some of these moments. But when those flashbacks of the experience persist and start to dominate a person's thinking, they need to be exorcised as much as possible. As the doulas listen to the dying story, they will hear obvious expressions of this type of pain or notice it on the fringes of what is said. Then they will seek ways to reframe those moments to lessen the negative impact on the grieving process.

Often the family does not take in or retain some of the more beautiful and loving moments that occurred during a vigil—a particularly moving expression of love, the tender caress of a loved one's cheek, an act of devotion toward another family member. The doulas give these moments back to family, which can then be woven into the fabric of their story to act as counterweights to the more painful moments. Sometimes, these touching moments become the most precious memories from the vigil.

For the last two days of Michael's life, his wife, Bridget, their two young daughters, and Bridget's brother hardly left the family room where Michael was dying. At night, the girls, ages fourteen and eleven, slept on blow-up beds; Bridget and her brother slept head to foot on the sectional couch.

During the vigil, the doulas came in shifts around the clock. They witnessed many acts of love and kindness that Bridget and her daughters didn't notice. At the only reprocessing session that the doulas did, they spoke about these very special moments.

"Bridget, I bet you don't remember this," said one of the doulas, "but at one point, Michael seemed agitated or uncomfortable. You climbed in the bed, lay right up against him, and wrapped your arms around him. After a few minutes, his body seemed to relax.

"Not only was that beautiful, but while you lay there, I happened to see your older daughter watching you. She had this amazing look on her face, one of sadness and happiness at the same time. I know she recognized in that moment how much you loved her father and did everything you could to take care of him.

"It was a wonderful example of how we should take care of people as they are dying, without awkwardness or fear. She will carry that into her adult life and remember it when she is faced with other deaths."

The doulas told more such stories involving Bridget and her daughters. Some stories involved Bridget's brother; some even involved their dog that came over and licked Michael's hand when his breathing really changed an hour before he died. When Michael took his last breath, Bridget and her daughters huddled together, holding one another fiercely at one side of the bed.

A doula who was there told it this way. "I will always remember your incredible strength, Bridget. You had just watched your husband take his last breath. But your entire focus was on the girls, making sure they remembered how much their father loved them. Then you told them he would always be with them in their hearts.

"They were both sobbing but nodding their heads and clinging to you and each other even more tightly. It was such a pure act of devotion and sacrifice on your part. You should be very proud of how you put yourself aside in those moments to take care of them."

When the reprocessing sessions begin, the grieving process has already started. Although people may still be in shock and numb, other elements of grief are seeping into their lives: the ups and downs of emotions, like riding a roller coaster in the dark; the inability to focus or concentrate; the sense of emptiness and loneliness; the questions about meaning and purpose; doubts about who they are, how they will go on, or how they can hold on to their faith; a sense of vulnerability.

The doulas can normalize this experience so that the family can understand that their responses to loss are a natural part of the grief process. Everyone must go through them to some extent, and probably for the next two to three years—sometimes longer. The doulas will also help the family understand how to cope with their grief and how to engage internally with the work that is necessary to heal well. This isn't grief counseling. This is an overview of the process so that family can see from an objective point of view what they have already begun to feel and what lies ahead.

The reprocessing work can move into more active early grief support if the family wants that kind of involvement. Only one or perhaps two of the doulas will conduct these sessions. They become companions in the family's grieving process. They walk alongside them in their emotions and responses in the same way they walked alongside them in the days of the vigil. The skills they use are also the same: deep active listening, touch, visualization, exploring meaning, working on a legacy.

Since grief is a long process, the doulas cannot stay involved the whole way. If they did, they would not be available to other dying people and their families. So, at some point, the work with the family must end. That might be after only one visit, or it might be after a few months. That is up to the family and the doulas.

Letting go is not generally easy for family members—or for the doulas. The bonds established during weeks or months of intimately working together, at an intense and very personal time, are quite powerful. Here ritual can play an important role. Ritual commemorates experiences; it signals the transition from one reality to another, and it allows the family and the doulas to say goodbye in a way that creates a positive sense of completion.

A ritual that ends the work of reprocessing may have been discussed way back at the time the vigil was planned. Or it can be created in the spur of the moment.

As it became clear that the reprocessing work with Steven's family was coming to its natural conclusion, the doulas discussed with them a ritual to end their involvement. Steven's wife, two grown children, and several grandchildren were to participate.

Since Steven's death, the family had kept a candle burning in front of a wicker basket that held the legacy messages family and friends had written to him before and during the vigil. For the ritual, the candle and basket were placed on a small table covered by a prayer shawl, one that Steven had worn when he went to temple for the High Holiday services each year. The table was surrounded by a large circle of chairs, placed so that the family and doulas could look at one another's faces at the same time that they faced the wicker basket.

In preparation for the ritual, the doulas wrote about a special moment during the vigil that touched them, some aspect of Steven's life they hoped the family would hold on to, or just their wishes for how the family would continue to heal in their grieving. When the time came, everyone gathered in the living room to sit on the chairs. The doulas held their messages folded in their laps.

As the ritual began, Steven's wife, Carol, put on a CD of Steven playing his guitar and singing songs he had written many years ago. Although Steven had been an engineer, he was also an amateur songwriter. Just hearing his voice brought tears to everyone's eyes. Carol then surprised the doulas by reading a letter that the family had written to them. The letter called the doulas "angels" and spoke about how important it had been to have them guide and assist the family through Steven's death. Every family member had signed the letter.

Next, the doulas took turns reading their messages, then went up to the table to place them in the wicker basket. Around the basket were rocks that Steven had collected during the long hikes he had taken in the woods of places he had traveled to over many years of his adult life. Each rock had been prized by him for its shape, color, exposed mineral vein, or an embedded fossil. When the doulas deposited their messages, they were each invited to take one of the rocks to keep in memory of Steven.

What made this part of the ritual so meaningful was that in the Jewish tradition, when you visit a person's grave, you are supposed to place a stone you find on the ground on top of the headstone or footstone. It shows that you visited.

Now each time a doula might look at the chosen rock, it would be as if Steven were visiting them. The messages the doulas left in the basket would later be tied together with a ribbon so that they would stay together as a group to be read at any time in the future by family or friends—along with all the other messages in the basket.

At the end of the ritual, Carol brought out wine—the very sweet red wine people drink at a Passover Seder. Everyone stood, raised their cup in a toast to Steven, and drank their wine. Finally, as they had planned, the doula who had facilitated the reprocessing meetings announced that this ended their work with the family, then snuffed out the candle.

Afterword

This book has been the culmination of twenty years of serving people who are dying and their families. It has been an incredible journey for me. I can honestly say that being a doula and teaching others to do this work have changed my life. It has also changed my perspective on dying.

While I can still touch inside me the primal fear of death that is part of our human survival instincts, I have come to see death as a gift. Death challenges us to find the best of who we are. It strips away everything that is unimportant and leaves what is essential. It opens us to great love, generosity, and courage.

Watching hundreds of people die has also proven to me a fundamental Buddhist teaching: impermanence is the nature of existence. And it is that truth that reminds us to live each moment as the only moment, surrendering over and over again as we prepare for the great surrender of death.

In the first end-of-life doula program I created, most of the ways we served the dying were a direct translation of the way birth

doulas serve a woman and her partner in labor. The main modi-
fication we had to make was using a team of doulas through the
labor of death, rather than just one doula, as in a birth. Since
the dying process can go on for as many as eight to ten days, it
would be impossible for one doula to stay around the clock. The
other reason for working in teams was that all the doulas were
volunteers.

Volunteerism is still at the heart of all the programs that
exist in hospices and hospitals today. But I see the early signs
of this changing, which I think is for the good of this growing
field. Birth doulas also began serving women without compen-
sation, but now, thirty-plus years or so later, they get paid for
doing their work—and in a couple of states their work is even
reimbursed by insurance. While I believe that some end-of-
life doula programs will remain volunteer-based, independent
groups of doulas will come to serve the dying in various ways
that provide them an income.

The work that doulas do at the end of life is also evolving with
time. The original program did very little to address meaning
and legacy with a dying person. Today, that work is a main focal
point of the model that I teach and help to establish in hospices,
hospitals, and communities.

Also, guided imagery plays a more important role in each
phase of the model. We use it to help a dying person and the
family envision what they believe would be a "good death" for
them. We use it to help a dying person achieve a greater sense
of well-being, manage symptoms, or work through spiritual distress. We use it as a way to reassure a dying person and help

guide them into the final process of letting go. We use it in the reprocessing work and build it into rituals.

We have also expanded the use of ritual. At first, we recognized that some of what we did right after a person died—almost without thinking about it—had the feel of ritual. But now we use ritual in a much more conscious way. We plan for it as we discuss with a dying person and the family their wishes for the vigil. We may conduct a ritual to begin a vigil, sometimes at the start or end of each day of a vigil, and of course right after the last breath. We have also incorporated ritual into the reprocessing work and use it to bring closure to our service with a family.

Certainly the work of end-of-life doulas will continue to evolve over time. For example, I now see closer linkages to the work of funeral directors that support people in having home viewings and funerals. After all, that is about ritual. The same is true in the use of "greener" forms of burial.

While we are still at the beginning of the movement toward a gentler, more meaningful death, I can already see signs that it is becoming part of the expanding conversation on death and dying in our society. The media has discovered this work. Almost every week, I come across or hear about another article, interview program, or documentary film devoted to the work that doulas do.

At the beginning of 2015, I cofounded the International End of Life Doula Association (INELDA), a nonprofit organization devoted to creating death doula programs in hospices, hospitals, and communities. INELDA also teaches individuals the approach and skills of the doula work and has created its own certification program to help establish a standard of professionalism in the field.

This is an exciting time that has brought us to the beginning of a new, meaningful way of death and dying. I hope that many of you who have now read this book will join in the work, or at least use what you have learned to help family and friends when they enter their dying process.

Acknowledgments

First and foremost, I would like to thank my wife, Stephanie, for her incredible love and support. She has been amazingly indulgent and patient with the crazy hours I sometimes keep and my absence from her, the family, and the normal routines of life. It hasn't been easy living with me. I can't imagine taking this journey with anyone else.

I want to thank my oldest son, Aron, for encouraging me and pushing me to "write my damn book already." And I want to thank my youngest son, Jared, for his company and questions in the middle of the night when I was writing the book.

I also have to thank—without naming—all the social workers, nurses, chaplains, birth doulas, and teachers of various kinds who have inspired me to do this work and helped me to learn what I needed to know.

Finally, I want to thank my cofounder in the International End of Life Doula Association (INELDA), Janie Rakow, and the many doulas who have given so much of their time to serve the dying. Your passion and devotion to the doula approach has changed many lives in remarkable ways. With all of your efforts, we will transform the way of dying in this culture and hopefully around the world.

To Our Readers

Conari Press, an imprint of Red Wheel/Weiser, publishes books on topics ranging from spirituality, personal growth, and relationships to women's issues, parenting, and social issues. Our mission is to publish quality books that will make a difference in people's lives—how we feel about ourselves and how we relate to one another. We value integrity, compassion, and receptivity, both in the books we publish and in the way we do business.

Our readers are our most important resource, and we appreciate your input, suggestions, and ideas about what you would like to see published.

Visit our website at *www.redwheelweiser.com* to learn about our upcoming books and free downloads, and be sure to go to *www.redwheelweiser.com/newsletter* to sign up for newsletters and exclusive offers.

You can also contact us at *info@rwwbooks.com.*

Conari Press
an imprint of Red Wheel/Weiser, LLC
65 Parker Street, Suite 7
Newburyport, MA 01950
www.redwheelweiser.com